LA GUARDIA
COMES
TO POWER

~⌒~ 1933 ~⌒~

BY ARTHUR MANN

PHOENIX BOOKS

THE UNIVERSITY OF CHICAGO PRESS

Chicago and London

THE UNIVERSITY OF CHICAGO PRESS, CHICAGO 60637
THE UNIVERSITY OF CHICAGO PRESS, LTD., LONDON W. C. 1
© 1965 by Arthur Mann. All rights reserved
Published by J. B. Lippincott Company 1965
First Phoenix Edition 1969
Printed in the United States of America

To Carol and Emily
with Love

Contents

Preface

This second installment of *La Guardia* is about how he became mayor of New York City in the regular municipal election of 1933 a year after Jimmy Walker had exiled himself to Europe in disgrace. As in the preceding volume I have tried through La Guardia to shed light on his times, and through his times to illuminate his significance. Yet it is not the book I originally planned to write or promised readers as a sequel to *A Fighter Against His Times*. A prefatory word is therefore doubly in order.

Volume one told La Guardia's story from 1882 just past 1932, and a second volume was supposed to carry it down to his death in 1947. The decision to divide the biography into those two parts rested on the fact that the chief turning point in La Guardia's public life was the mayoralty. Before then he lived on the edges of power and fought the establishment—hence the title of the first volume: *A Fighter Against His Times*. But through the mayoralty La Guardia joined the liberal political establishment of the 1930's and 1940's to move and deal with some of the most important political leaders of his generation. My intention in the second volume was to ask how and how well La Guardia used power and for what purposes.

But in doing the research and—more importantly—in the process of writing, I realized that another question claimed priority. How did La Guardia, in the first instance, come to power in 1933? I had known, of course, that I would have to answer the question, but like so many New Yorkers who grew up in the Mayor's city, I had taken for granted his being chief executive (who of my generation can imagine the 1930's and 1940's without the Little Flower?). To take men and events for granted is only a short step from accepting them as inevitable, and I thought that I would be able to dispose of the election of 1933 in an opening chapter and then get into those years when, Rexford Tugwell has written, only the President of the United States was better known as an American political leader than the Mayor of New York.

The chapter I started out to write grew into the book now in your hands. Hard as I tried to cut it in successive drafts, certain details couldn't be condensed without losing their flavor or blurring their connections. La Guardia's triumph in 1933 wasn't in the least inevitable, I discovered; it hung on a series of turning points, each of which had to be passed for the final outcome to be achieved. I therefore decided to devote an entire volume to La Guardia's coming to power. It is a story worth telling in its own right, I believe, and also as a case study of how the political guard is changed in a fantastically heterogeneous society. A self-governing people cannot know too much about that process; and New York City, its critics to the contrary, is America.

For the benefit of readers unfamiliar with the preceding volume, or whose memory of it has dimmed, I have recapitulated in parts of Chapter I facts about La Guardia's early life relevant to the narrative of this book. A third installment will, hopefully, conclude a series that both my publisher and I had envisioned in 1955 as a mere 150,000-word political biography.

Once again it is a pleasure to thank a number of men and women who took time out of their busy lives to reminisce with me in person or writing (some did both) about their memories of La Guardia. They include Joey Adams, Harry G. Andrews, Dr. George Baehr, the Reverend Gerald V. Barry, August Bellanca, Giuseppe Bellanca, Adolf A. Berle, Edward L. Bernays, Francis J. Bloustein, Mrs. Walter G. Bunzl, Charles Culp Burlingham, Eugene R. Canudo, Anthony Capraro, Edward Corsi, Henry H. Curran, Louis Espresso, Dominick P. Felitti, Lewis Gannett, Frank Giordano, Gemma La Guardia Gluck, J. Owen Grundy, Fannie Hurst, Paul J. Kern, Jean La Guardia, Marie F. La Guardia, Reuben A. Lazarus, Philip J. McCook, Rufus E. McGahen, Joseph D. McGoldrick, W. Kingsland Macy, Chase Mellen, Jr., Emily P. Mikszto, Newbold

Morris, Robert Moses, Edmund L. Palmieri, Maurice G. Postley, Victor F. Ridder, Harry N. Rosenfield, Domenick M. Rufolo, Onorio Ruotolo, Dudley F. Sicher, Lee Thompson Smith, Francis R. Stoddard, Frederick C. Tanner, Norman Thomas, P. Tozzi, Mrs. M. L. Tribby, Charles H. Tuttle, Louis M. Weintraub, Paul Windels, and Keyes Winter.

It is now ten years since research for this biography began, and during that decade three men of the La Guardia circle in particular have sustained me and encouraged me to go on. They are the Honorable Adolf A. Berle, Judge Eugene R. Canudo, and Commissioner Newbold Morris. Neither they nor I anticipated that this project would take so much time. Their patience has made me less self-conscious than I otherwise might be about my slowness. And their loyalty to La Guardia's memory notwithstanding, they have appreciated the responsibility I have of telling La Guardia's story as a non-partisan. This volume, like the preceding one, is my own, not an "official" biography.

However much this book rests on live sources, it rests still more on the resources of libraries. Through Miss Margaret L. Johnson, Librarian of the William Allan Neilson Library of Smith College, and Mr. Edward G. Freehafer, Director of the Forty-second Street Library of New York City, I have been able to use the La Guardia Papers at my own convenience. Mr. James Katsaros, Administrator of the Municipal Archives and Records Center, expedited that process and has been helpful in many other ways. To Eugene Bockman, who heads the Municipal Reference Library, I express gratitude for services cheerfully given. Dr. Louis Starr, and the staff he directs on the Columbia University Oral History Project, kindly assisted me through their important and still growing collection of reminiscences. Robert W. Hill, Keeper of the Manuscripts, the New York Public Library, Mr. John D. Stinson, and Miss Elizabeth M. Eilerman of the Municipal Archives and Records Center located and checked, on short notice, the accuracy of important quotations in this book.

Adolf A. Berle, Lewis Gannett, and Frederick C. Tanner allowed me the use of certain of their personal files, while Reuben A. Lazarus and Paul Windels permitted me to read their unpublished memoirs. Frank and Robert Davidson kindly called my attention to and invited me to use the papers of their father, Maurice P. Davidson. To my colleague, Professor William E. Leuchtenburg, I owe a debt for items sent from the Milo Reno and Franklin D. Roosevelt manuscripts.

A fellowship from the American Council of Learned Societies enabled me to finance a sabbatical leave in the academic year 1962–1963 to crack the back of the book. Grants-in-aid from the Social Science Research Council and the Smith College Committee on Faculty Research covered much of the expense involved over the years. I am sincerely grateful to all three institutions.

To the many Smith College students who assisted me in different ways and at various times, I say thanks to one and all, and beg of them not to consider it invidious if I single out by name Jane L. Rockman and Nancy J. Weiss of the class of 1965. Working with me on the final stages of preparing the manuscript, they made it possible for me to present the book to the public this year.

Five colleagues who are also friends—Professors Daniel Aaron, Stanley Elkins, Oscar Handlin, Peter d'A. Jones, and Donald Sheehan—read *La Guardia Comes to Power* in manuscript and called my attention to errors in fact, interpretation, and style. The errors that remain belong to me. Miss Anita Pertz translated the Yiddish- and German-language press for me, while Mrs. Kathleen Lord deciphered my writing for the benefit of the printer. In the final process of revision, I profited considerably from the editorial help of Robert D. Mead and George Stevens of Lippincott.

My wife already knows how much I owe her. But I have often wondered if my two daughters, now thirteen and sixteen, have ever realized what they have contributed to THE BOOK. Although absorbed in their own problems in growing up, they took an interest in those of mine connected with La Guardia. For their concern, and warmth and affection and gaiety, I cannot thank them enough.

ARTHUR MANN

Northampton,
Massachusetts

LA GUARDIA COMES TO POWER:
1933

I

"Now We Have a Mayor of New York!"

Fiorello H. La Guardia was sworn in as the ninety-ninth Mayor of New York City at a few minutes past midnight on January 1, 1934. The inauguration ceremony took place in the library of Judge Samuel Seabury's town house, 154 East Sixty-third Street, and was attended by Mrs. La Guardia, a handful of old friends, and leaders of the reform coalition that in November had voted Tammany out of City Hall. One wonders what Seabury's patrician ancestors, whose portraits looked down on the ceremony from the walls of the elegant library, would have thought of the political partnership between their descendant and a rough-and-tumble professional politician who had been born of immigrant parents in a tenement. After the Little Flower took the oath of office from State Supreme Court Justice Philip J. McCook (who in 1910 had helped a fledgling attorney rent his first law office in a closet-sized room at 15 William Street in lower Manhattan), Seabury exclaimed:

"Now we have a Mayor of New York!"[1]

1. *"To the Victor Belongs the Responsibility for Good Government"*

Mayor La Guardia turned out to be the greatest showman, the most accomplished political impresario, and the least inhibited chief executive ever to occupy City Hall. No other American politician of his time, with the exception of Franklin D. Roosevelt, made so much news. Merely to list his activities required more than two hundred and fifty double-column pages in the *Index* to the New York *Times*. It was news when His Honor raced his own firemen to fires, or when he conducted the New York Philharmonic Orchestra while Toscanini looked on approvingly, or when he read the comics over the radio to the kiddies, or when he nominated Adolf Hitler for membership in an international chamber of horrors.

The public scarcely knew a dull moment while the bouncy, irrepressibly irreverent Little Flower was around. His humor could be broad and sly. Once, when asked under what authority he proposed to ban the sale of dirty magazines in the city, he explained, grinning, that "the Mayor has power of sewage," and then had himself photographed pushing a Department of Sanitation broom. His humor could also be biting and ironical. In complying with a request from the German Consulate in New York City for police protection against possible retaliation by Jews infuriated over Nazi atrocities in Germany, La Guardia selected for that duty a crack contingent of Jewish cops. There was also a brutal and sadistic side to his humor. The Mayor once summoned a commissioner to his office for doing something wrong and then called for a stenographer just so that he could shout at her: "If you were any dumber, I'd make you a commissioner."

So much about him had a touch of the extravagant, the improbable, the tall story, the incongruous, and even the outrageous. Out of such stuff Americans have created their folk heroes. La Guardia was one of them. A legendary figure during his own lifetime, he was idolized, and still is in some quarters, as a combination of Paul Bunyan, Jim Bowie, and Davy Crockett, New York style; he was the half-horse, half-alligator superman who defended the Alamo (read City Hall) against the Tammany Tiger. The legends about him since his death in 1947 have multiplied (he has been memorialized in stained-glass in one New York Episcopal church), and there is a danger that the historical La Guardia will be sacrificed to the mythological Little Flower.[2]

This is all the more unfortunate because the historical La Guardia was so full of improbabilities that there is no need to embellish them. Therein lies the fun and the fascination of Fiorello. It was hard to believe that he had been raised in Arizona, for he spoke with an unmistakable New York accent and punctuated his speech with exuberant Latin gestures. Nominally a Republican, he campaigned for the Democratic Roosevelt in 1936, yet the following year he won the support of Roosevelt-hating Republicans for his own re-election. Even in polyglot Gotham, where exotic human varieties were limitless, the mind balked at an Italo-Jewish-American Episcopalian Mayor with a Lutheran wife of German descent.

That someone of his size, shape, and sound should have been a leader of men was the most extraordinary thing of all. Only five feet two, he was as corpulent as he was short. If he neglected to dress well, it was because he recognized that no tailor, no matter how ingenious, could change him into a fine figure of a man. To look at his heavy, round, jowly face, one would think that his voice would be deep and perhaps resonant. It was neither and sounded like an older choir boy's tenor-alto. When the Mayor got angry, moreover, he shrieked. Under the wide brim of his black Stetson, his trademark, he looked like a vaudeville comedian when gay, or if stern, like an elder statesman of the Lucky Luciano mob.

Yet he was a leader of men, as everyone knows; in fact, the outstanding municipal leader of his generation and the best mayor New York City has had. He did what no New York City mayor had done before or has done since: he proved that one could be an authentic reformer without being a stuffed shirt or a fool about political realities. Unlike his well-bred, frock-coated, reform predecessors in City Hall, La Guardia succeeded himself in office, winning re-election in 1937 and again in 1941. And he knew how to use power, as well as how to gain and retain it. He changed the physical appearance of his city for the good; he improved its administration in a multitude of ways; he set an example for municipal achievement in health, housing, recreation, protection, planning, and even the arts. The airport that bears his name is only one of many monuments he left behind him.

Tammany Hall, battered by La Guardia and starved for patronage by the New Deal, was forced in 1943 to sell the Wigwam, the gorgeous clubhouse it had built in 1929 on Union Square, and to move into plainer quarters in another part of town. No other event symbolized better the transformation of New York's political scene during the La Guardia years (1934–1945). In 1940 Yale University awarded an honorary doctorate to the man who had neither a high-school diploma nor an undergraduate degree.* "He has taken democracy away from the politicians," the citation read, "and restored it to the people."[3]

But when he made his first bid for the mayoralty back in 1921, La Guardia could remember that his own Republican boss of Manhattan, Sam Koenig, had tried to dissuade him from entering the Republican primary in these words: "Don't do it, Fiorello. The town isn't ready for an Italian mayor."[4] La Guardia, then president of the Board of Aldermen, was confident that Koenig was wrong. He ran in the primary, but was derided by the Republican press as "the little Garibaldi" and "OUR OWN LITTLE STROMBOLI," and failed to carry a single borough. And back in 1929, La Guardia could also remember, he forced the nomination from party leaders, many of whom then sat out the campaign or actively helped the Democratic incumbent, Jimmy Walker, to humiliate "the crazy little wop" in the worst defeat of his political career. Fiorello lost every one of the city's sixty-two assembly districts.

Because New York City's municipal elections were held in odd-numbered years, La Guardia had been able to run for mayor without resigning the congressional seat he had won in 1922 and had retained since then. By 1932 even that was gone. In the national election of that year his East Harlem district, which he had brilliantly represented in the nation's capital for a decade, repudiated him in favor of an ingratiating Tammany candidate, James J. Lanzetta, who was soon to vanish into the obscurity from which he had emerged. Heartbroken and

---

* La Guardia earned an LL.B from New York University's law school, where he attended classes, mostly in the evening session, from 1907 to 1910.

bewildered, but only temporarily, the defeated Congressman journeyed to Washington for the lame-duck session of the Seventy-second Congress. When his term was over and he came back to New York City in March of 1933, his political future looked bleaker than ever before. Not only was he out of a political job; he seemed to be a loser.

It is therefore understandable that Fiorello should have felt particularly good when, on that 1934 New Year's Eve, he stood in Judge Seabury's library surrounded by the more important architects of the first successful Fusion movement since the election of John P. Mitchel in 1913. Seabury and C. C. (Charles Culp) Burlingham, whose progressive records went back to the late nineteenth century, were the most eminent spokesmen of an older generation of municipal reformers. Maurice P. Davidson, head of the recently created City Fusion Party, represented the newer generation. The ranking New Dealer of the La Guardia coalition, Professor A. A. Berle, Jr., was a Roosevelt brain truster. The leading Republican of that coalition was W. Kingsland Macy, New York State chairman of the Republican Party. Roy Howard, publisher of the New York *World-Telegram*, was there for the liberal newspaper world. At least a half dozen other men of similar caliber attended the inauguration.[5] Never before had La Guardia been honored by so many public figures of such renown.

Not only had his career been miraculously retrieved at the zero hour, but what he had stood for and fought for had been vindicated. The humbling of his enemies was complete. Tammany's contribution to the Jazz Age, former Mayor Jimmy ("Beau James") Walker, had fled the country in disgrace and was living in exile with his mistress. The Democratic machine, its arrogance and monolithic power shattered by the campaign of 1933, would need some twelve years before it could put all its parts together again. As for the Republican Party, its leaders had reason to fear where they stood with the emotional little fellow who remembered that they had contributed substantially to making him a two-time loser. Now, as a winner, he was the master of policy and patronage in a city whose budget was second in America only to that of the Federal Government.

Mrs. La Guardia also felt vindicated. For twenty years, first as a secretary and then as a wife, she had fought beside him. In her *Reminiscences* she wrote this about La Guardia's finally becoming mayor: "It was like he owned the United States. Nobody should do anything to it."

La Guardia kissed his wife after taking the oath of office, then stepped up to a microphone rigged up by the newsreel companies. "The Fusion administration is now in charge of our city," he said in his high-pitched voice. "Our theory of municipal government is an experiment, to try to show that a nonpartisan, non-political local government is possible. . . ." The eyes of America were on New York, for "if we succeed," La Guardia concluded, "I am sure success in other cities is possible."

That's all there was to the inauguration. There were no parades, no brass bands, no striped pants. Seabury and other guests, accustomed to appearing at evening functions in evening clothes, were dressed in tuxedos; but La Guardia wore an ordinary business suit. It was neatly pressed, visibly so, which suggests that the Mayor (or his wife) had made at least one sartorial concession to the occasion. They did not linger after the ceremony; La Guardia went home to bed so that he could get a good night's rest before reporting for his new job.[6]

His inauguration was the simplest, the shortest, the quietest, the most earnest, and the most functional in the history of the New York mayoralty. These are not the qualities one usually associates with the La Guardia razzmatazz. But it is often forgotten that he had range, the most exacting test of showmanship and of intelligence as well. The no-nonsense character of his investiture dramatized the slogan of his incoming administration:

"To the victor belongs the responsibility for good government."[7]

He assumed that responsibility immediately. At 8:30 A.M., January 1, 1934, La Guardia strode from the East Harlem apartment house where he lived in a simply furnished flat and entered a limousine bearing the Mayor's official five-star shield. Many of his townsmen were still asleep, recovering from the first legally wet New Year's Eve in fourteen years, or else on holiday. La Guardia sped downtown to work. When he

returned home that night at half past six, there was no doubt
about who was running the government of New York City.

After first addressing two hundred ranking officers at Police
Headquarters ("Drive out the racketeers," he warned, "or get
out yourselves") he descended on City Hall. Three stenogra-
phers took his rapid-fire dictation as he raced through a pile of
correspondence with such ejaculations as "Nuts," "Regrets,"
"Thanks,"—"Where's the waste basket! . . . That's going to
be the most important file around City Hall." Fuming over the
number of telephones and jumble of wires on his desk, he
exploded: "One's enough, I can't work with all that junk
around."

So it went on that first day: action, then more action, and
still more action. "Clean house and clean it thoroughly," he
ordered his cabinet members as he swore them in. He informed his Corporation Counsel: "I don't care whether the
Law Department is the biggest law office in the world. I want
it to be the best." He commanded his Commissioner of Cor-
rections: "Remove every one from top to bottom, if necessary
to straighten out this department. . . ." He told his Commissioner of Taxes: "There's something wrong in the Tax Department, but I don't know just what it is. See if you can find
out."

At 11:15 A.M. he delivered his inaugural address from the
National Broadcasting Company studio. He called attention to
"these times of stress and trouble," promised to co-operate
with President Roosevelt and Governor Lehman, and dramatically concluded by taking the Oath of the Young Men of
Athens:

> We will never bring disgrace to this, our city, by any act
> of dishonesty or cowardice nor ever desert our suffering com-
> rades in the ranks. We will fight for our ideals and sacred
> things of the city, both alone and with many. We will revere
> and obey the city's laws and do our best to incite a like
> respect in those above us who are prone to annul them and
> set them at naught. We will strive unceasingly to quicken the
> public sense of civic duty. Thus in all these ways we will
> transmit this city not only not less but far greater and more
> beautiful than it was transmitted to us.

He returned to his desk after a lunch that was something of a munch. There were more letters to attend to, more commissioners to see, more orders to give, more speeches. In his opening address to the Board of Aldermen, which was controlled by hostile Democrats, La Guardia demanded that they support his plan to avert bankruptcy by slashing salaries and removing leeches from the public payroll. When the Democrats declared that their function as the majority was to lead and not to follow, the Mayor retorted: "I'm the majority in this administration."

His energy, after years of Tammany lethargy, won unanimous editorial praise. "You've got to hand it, we'd say, to Mayor Fiorello H. La Guardia for the way he went about taking charge of New York City," commented the *Daily News*. The municipal government was on the move again, as La Guardia had promised it would be under his direction. "Good work, Mr. Mayor!" exclaimed the Brooklyn *Times Union*. "You have made a grand start." Not even the opposition press could find fault with La Guardia on his first day in office. He had captured the entire city by the simple dignity of his inauguration in Judge Seabury's home, his startling appearance at his desk on New Year's Day, his theatrical flourish in reciting the Athenian Oath, and his speed and decisiveness in changing the Old Guard and installing the new.

"Probably never before did a mayor of New York," the New York *Times* summed up the case, "begin his term with such an air of swiftly getting down to business and enforcing industry and honesty on the part of every municipal employee."[8]

If praise for La Guardia was extravagant on the cold January first of 1934, it was partly because New York was very ready for a change that would restore its self-confidence. He took office not only in the midst of a terrible depression but after a decade and more of cynical misrule. The gang that had misgoverned the city had made bribery, wire-pulling, and influence-peddling into a way of life, from fixing a lowly traffic ticket all the way up to buying a judgeship. By 1934 the city's credit was so badly impaired that municipal securities were selling twenty-six points under par. Public funds were nearly exhausted for almost half a million persons on relief. Many departments suffered from incompetence, corruption, and low morale. Numerous unfinished public works, like the Triborough Bridge, stood as grim monuments to the Tammany credo: the public be damned, "I seen my opportunities and I took 'em."[9]

Across the seas, free government was threatened not by the perversion of the democratic creed, but by totalitarianism. The Fascist dictator of Italy, an exponent of harsh discipline since the early 1920's, would soon send troops to conquer Ethiopia and topple the Spanish Republic. Already the Japanese military junto had overrun Manchuria. In the Soviet Union Lenin's successor directed a world-wide apparatus against bourgeois liberalism. One year before La Guardia's inauguration a former paperhanger from Austria became the Chancellor of Germany and the hangman of the Weimar Republic. In the United States the New Deal had not yet proved, by 1934, that an open society could cope with the massive disorders of the Depression and still remain open.

Clearly, La Guardia had assumed a fateful responsibility. He belonged to the generation of Hirohito and Stalin, of Mussolini and Hitler and Franco, of Roosevelt and Churchill. That the Mayor had little to do with foreign affairs does not diminish his importance. The 1930's and 1940's were a testing ground for the principles, the ingenuity, the institutions, and the leadership of representative government. New York, the biggest city in the largest democracy on the globe, was in 1934 embarking, in La Guardia's words, on an experiment.

What qualities had the Mayor shown *before* 1934 that qualified him for leadership in so critical a period for his city, his country, and his world?

2. *Hybridism, Power, Conscience*

Some men go to the top in politics when society seems to be a going concern and the people have need of an amiable figurehead who is content to stand still. It is usual for such a leader to avoid conflict, stress harmony, and celebrate what is: to assure and reassure the electorate that they've never had it so good. Government is not supposed to be an instrument for social change, it is considered an exercise in caretaking. Such is the leadership of normalcy.

Neither by temperament nor intellect was La Guardia the sort to administer a going concern. Unable to slow down long enough to stand still, he was inclined to shock and mock the celebrators of the status quo and to celebrate only the possibilities of the future. He throve on conflict, not harmony, in situations that made reform possible. It was no accident that the Anti-Injunction Act,* for which La Guardia and Senator George Norris had agitated futilely during the so-called normalcy of the 1920's, should suddenly have been passed by Congress at the beginning of the Depression. Fiorello was the kind of leader who comes into his own when a crisis in the old order creates opportunities for new directions.

Yet the laws of heredity and environment that produce a La Guardia have still to be discovered. His biographer can only call attention to his most important characteristics, infer their probable source from available evidence, and relate them to the culture in which they flourished. Three characteristics of the fifty-one-year-old man who entered City Hall in 1934 deserve special mention and elaboration: his hybridism, his ambition for power and fame, and his passion to do good.

His hybridism derived from an extraordinary mobility. Born in Greenwich Village but raised on Western Army posts and growing to maturity in the Balkans, he returned to his native city at twenty-three and later spent much of his adult life in the nation's capital as a Congressman. All his life he had been learning how to live in someone else's culture and he acquired a working knowledge of half a dozen languages besides English: Italian, French, German, Yiddish, Hungarian, and Serbo-Croatian. He was a true cosmopolitan, which is to say that he

---

* This milestone in social legislation, which President Hoover signed on March 23, 1932, restated the right of workingmen to bargain collectively and also declared that government had the responsibility to help them do so. Among other provisions, the Norris–La Guardia Act forbade Federal courts to issue injunctions against a strike or against peaceful activities to carry on a strike unless the employer could prove that he had tried to settle the strike, been threatened, or that the strike would cause him irreparable harm.

was at home nearly everywhere, but without the roots that bind a true insider to the group and the place in which he was born.

His parentage foreordained that he would be what sociologists call a marginal man. Achille Luigi Carlo La Guardia and his wife Irene Coen emigrated to America in 1880 and returned to Italy with their children twenty years later. Theirs was a mixed marriage—Achille was a lapsed Catholic and Irene a lukewarm Jew—and while in the United States they raised their children as Episcopalians. When, in 1906, Fiorello returned to America, where everyone has an ethnic label or gets one, he considered himself an Italo-American. But his being a Protestant set him apart from his ethnic group, which was, of course, overwhelmingly Catholic.

Observers have asked why Fiorello did not identify himself as a Jew. His inheritance is again instructive. Irene Coen La Guardia, his Trieste-born mother, thought of herself as Austrian in nationality, Italian in culture, and Jewish only in religion. There was no Jewish community in the army towns where Fiorello grew up while his father was serving in the United States Army as a bandmaster. When Fiorello met Jews in large numbers—first as a consular agent in Fiume, then as an Ellis Island interpreter, and later as a labor lawyer on Manhattan's Lower East Side—he met Jews unlike his mother. They were Eastern European, not Mediterranean, Jews. They spoke Yiddish, their ritual was Ashkenazic, and they considered themselves a nationality and a cultural group as well as a religious body. Neither by descent nor religious upbringing was Fiorello one of them.

Nor was it expedient for him to be be known as Jewish when he broke into politics in the 1910's. He started out with handicaps enough against him. His aberrant appearance and unpronounceable name put him at a disadvantage to the dominant Celtic and the vanishing Anglo-Saxon types who ran the city. Nativism was rising and would shortly culminate in restrictive legislation against the new immigrants from eastern and southern Europe. It was hard enough to be an Italo-American fifty and more years ago without inviting the derisive taunt—which his enemies would hurl at him in the 1930's after his mother's origins became known—"the half-Jewish wop."

So he made little of his Jewish background in public but exploited his Italian name and built a political base in Little Italy from which to launch a career. By 1934 not even Primo Carnera or Benito Mussolini exceeded the Little Flower as a popular idol in the colony. What is more, after establishing his public image as a Latin he championed a number of Jewish causes, sometimes in Yiddish, but as an understanding and compassionate *outsider*. This was smart politics in the largest Jewish city in the world (the Jews and the Italians together constituted almost 45 per cent of New York's population in the 1920's and 1930's). It was also, and nevertheless, sincere. Free from self-hatred, La Guardia was a man of mixed loyalties.

The son of Jewish and Italian immigrants who attended services in the Cathedral of Saint John the Divine, but who was married to his first wife in the rectory of Saint Patrick's and to his second wife by a Lutheran minister, was clearly the most remarkable hybrid in the history of New York City politics. Belonging, yet not fully belonging, to nearly every important ancestral group in the city, including the British-descended community of Episcopalians, Fiorello was a balanced ticket all by himself.[10]

His being marginal to many cultures had a deeper significance still. The mayor of New York, like the leader of any pluralist community, must be a political broker. This had been a familiar role to the hyphenated Congressman who started his career on the Lower East Side as a mediator between immigrant and native America, interpreting one to the other. A friend in court for the poor and the persecuted, he also had served as a go-between for reformers and professional politicians and a bridge connecting urban and rural progressives in Congress.* The mayoralty would enlarge the scope of previous experience. La Guardia would have to balance the demands of a variety of competing interest groups in the city, and also

---

* John A. Simpson, president of the National Farmers' Union, described La Guardia to a colleague in these words: "Coming right out of the heart of the biggest city in the United States, . . . [he had] a sympathy and an understanding of farm problems that surpassed most of the Congressmen from agricultural districts." Simpson to Milo Reno, April 25, 1933, Milo Reno MSS. (privately held).

bargain and trade with borough, county, state, and Federal officials whose power impinged on his own as chief executive.[11]

But an effective leader must not only mediate and negotiate, he also has to command, take the initiative, make policy, and break through channels when necessary to get things done. Such a leader seeks power, enlarges it, and enjoys its use. La Guardia was like that by 1934. One of the few pieces of sculpture the Mayor owned was a bust of Napoleon that he first put on his desk when he began to practice law at twenty-eight. When he bought that object is unknown, but Bonaparte may have been his model at an even earlier age.

"Ambitious for promotion"—that is how the American Consul General of Budapest, who was given to the understatement of his New England birth and education, described his Italo-American subordinate in Fiume at the turn of the century. Commissioned a consular agent at twenty-one, Fiorello's pride of rank was inordinate. He expanded his jurisdiction whenever possible, breaking archaic rules and bringing them up to date on his own authority. The results of his innovations were often salutary, but his aggressiveness antagonized superiors. He quit in a huff after two and a half years, writing in 1906 to the State Department "that the service is not the place for a young man to work up. . . ."[12]

During World War I, as a major in command of American aviation in Italy, La Guardia was something of a virtuoso in running around, over, across, or simply straight through the protocol of two armies and one foreign government. Not having resigned his seat in Congress, he either impressed or intimidated higher ranking officers with his political connections. And forced to improvise on America's forgotten front, he improvised brilliantly, whether in training pilots, conferring with cabinet ministers, speeding up the production of planes, or rallying Italians to their own war effort after the disaster of Caporetto. "I love him like a brother," one Italian official exclaimed.[13]

Many voters in America felt much the same way. Between 1914 and 1934 La Guardia ran for office twelve times, and apart from a first and hopeless try, he lost only twice. His

victories were particularly impressive in view of the fact that
New York City was virtually a one-party (Democratic) town.
Elected president of the Board of Aldermen in 1919, he was
the first Republican to win a city-wide contest without Fusion
backing since the creation of Greater New York by legislative
act in 1897.* At one time during the 1920's La Guardia was the
sole Republican Congressman from Manhattan outside the silk-
stocking district.

His most obvious asset as a campaigner was his grasp of
relevant issues and his ability to dramatize those issues, and
himself as well, in colorful language and forceful terms. And
once in office he was conscientious in serving his constituents.
He was particularly popular with immigrants and their children, who accounted for 75 per cent of New York's population when he was rising to power. He was fighting their
battle, and his, too, for recognition and against bigotry. One of
the few ethnic groups that could not claim the multi-hyphen-
ated Little Flower through blood were the Polish-Americans,
yet *Nowy Swiat*, a Polish-language newspaper, looked up to
him as "head of the family . . . father, leader, judge, authority, and educator—like in the village. . . ."

But there was a Machiavellian, even diabolical, side to La
Guardia's melting-pot politics. When haranguing an audience,
which he could do in any of seven languages, he was not above
exploiting its fears, insecurities, prejudices, and hatreds. There
were ways and ways of getting out the vote. After one such a
harangue to an Italo-American crowd in the campaign of 1919,
he turned in pride to an associate and said: "I can outdemagogue the best of demagogues."[14]

He justified such tactics by insisting that he had to fight the
Tammany Tiger with its own weapons, and it was said of the
Little Flower during his life that he was no shrinking violet.
What a negative way of putting it! Fiorello was a superbly
conditioned political animal who not only struck back when

* New York City was simply Manhattan until the annexation of the
west Bronx in 1874. The rest of the Bronx was annexed in 1895, and
two years later a state law added Brooklyn, Queens, and Staten Island.
Today's boundaries of the city are identical with those established in
1897.

attacked but who really enjoyed the brutal struggle for office in the Manhattan jungle. No matter what he said in public to the contrary, La Guardia was a professional politician, bruising, cunning, tough, and with a strong stomach for the sordid methods and grubby details of election politics in his part of the world. "I invented the low blow," he boasted to an aide in the 1920's.[15] In East Harlem, which he represented in Congress for five terms until 1932, he commanded a superb personal organization of his own and gave lessons to Tammany at election time in machine campaigning.

The Mayor knew how to get power, all right, and how to keep it, as his record for election and re-election proves. But why did he want it? There are very many gifted men, after all, for whom public responsibility is distasteful and whose main thrust is for money, leisure, travel, or women. Those had been the tastes of Mayor Jimmy Walker, who gladly let the Tammany bosses govern New York City while he relentlessly pursued pleasure on two continents.

Some of La Guardia's associates thought, and still think, that in reaching out for power he was compensating for feelings of inferiority deriving from a hypersensitivity to his size, his lack of formal education, and his origins. To reduce the complexity of Fiorello's behavior to an inferiority complex is too pat and too simple. His wife, who knew him as well as anyone, has dismissed the idea as preposterous. Yet it is a matter of historical record that the Little Flower *was* hypersensitive and, therefore, easily insulted and ferociously combative.

Who can forget the fury, for example, with which the Mayor banned organ-grinders from the streets of New York? Those foreign-looking men, with their broken English, farcical little monkeys, and panhandling canned music, called attention to one of several disreputable Italian stereotypes that the Little Flower had labored all his life to refute and overcome. And although he himself might joke about his height and that of other men, no one else was allowed to do so in his presence. Once, when an associate made the mistake of being playful about a pint-sized applicant for a municipal job, La Guardia lost control of himself and screamed:

"What's the matter with a little guy? What's the matter with a little guy? What's the matter with a little guy?"[16]

The Mayor was clearly a man of explosive resentments. They were long-standing and are a key to his personality. As a boy growing up on army posts he had resented the children of officers for lording it over the children of enlisted men. Why was he not as good as they? Later, in the Foreign Service or in the Army, on the Board of Aldermen or in Congress, he would resent superiors he thought intellectually and morally inferior to himself. By what rights should they be placed over him? To measure one's self against others is normal for competitive men, but in La Guardia's case it was excessive. His resentfulness heightened his competitiveness and his competitiveness intensified his resentfulness, so that he was constantly in rivalry with nearly everyone he met and forever proving that he was number one.

"I think he put on a great deal of his brutalities to test people out," C. C. Burlingham, who knew La Guardia well, has shrewdly observed. "If they could stand up against him it was all right, but if they couldn't they were in bad luck."[17]

That La Guardia was ambitious will surprise only those people who think that a stained-glass window of Saint Francis is really a sufficient monument to the Mayor's memory. Yet only a mistaken realism would conclude that there was nothing more to his nature, and to human nature in general, than the promotion of self. Ed Flynn, the Democratic boss from the Bronx who prided himself on being a realistic judge of men, made that kind of mistake.[18] That is why Flynn was never able to understand and appreciate—or cope with—the *direction* of La Guardia's drive.

The direction was a liberal one. La Guardia wanted the power of public office not just to assert himself, it must be emphasized, but so that he could also be in a position to right social wrongs. Joining his resentments to a cause, he made a career for himself as a leader of the have-nots against the haves, or as he would have put it, the People against the Interests.

That was the image he had of himself—when he strove as a consul agent and interpreter to defend the humanity of immigrants against bureaucratic mindlessness and heartlessness; when he contributed his services as a lawyer and an orator to the trade unions that began to emerge in the 1910's from the squalid sweatshops of the Lower East Side; when as an over-age aviator he went off to war to make the world safe for democracy; when as president of the Board of Aldermen he defied the governor of New York State and fought against an increase of the five-cent fare on the subway (the poor man's ride) and the repeal of the direct primary (the people's defense against bossism); when as a Republican Congressman he bolted his party to join the Progressive Party of 1924 in a crusade against the credo of the day that the business of America was business, not welfare. Had La Guardia done nothing else he still would have passed the bar of American liberalism in 1934 for the anti-injunction law he co-authored two years earlier with Nebraska's Senator Norris; it was the most significant piece of labor legislation passed by Congress up to that time.

La Guardia entered City Hall with a sense of injustice that was still bottomless, with a capacity for outrage that was still boundless, with a determination to reform society that was still enormous. His social conscience was as highly developed as his instinct for the jugular in political combat. The mayor's office, toward which he had reached out three times before finally capturing it, would give him the power he had wanted so long in order to realize his humanitarian goals.

The thrust of an enormous internal drive to establish his own high place in the sum of things carried La Guardia very close to the top in American politics, and in that process he found more gratification in public fame than in the pleasures of private life.

When Fiorello returned to New York in 1906 after resigning from the consular service in Fiume ("Look here, Mother," he said in explanation, "I'm going back to America to become a lawyer and make something of myself."),[19] he arrived without friends or family. His father had been dead for two years and his mother chose to remain in Europe with her married daughter. The next decade and a half were devoted to the struggle to gain a foothold in the city he would someday rule.

Not until 1919, when he was thirty-six, back from the wars as a hero, and finally established in his career, did Congressman La Guardia take a wife, an exquisite young blonde from Trieste by the name of Thea Almerigotti.

That marriage was, and would remain, the high point of La Guardia's private emotional experience. Setting up housekeeping in Greenwich Village, the couple enjoyed a semi-Bohemian life, one that was full of love and fun and music and good eating. La Guardia adored children, and in 1920 Thea gave birth to a daughter, who was named Fioretta after Fiorello's maternal grandmother. Yet La Guardia's personal happiness flickered for only a moment. Throughout 1921 he suffered the agony of watching his baby, and then his wife, waste away and die of tuberculosis. For the next eight years he threw himself into his work with an energy that can only be described as ferocious.

His second marriage in 1929 to Marie Fischer, his secretary since 1914, was a union of two mature persons. It was not blessed with children. The couple adopted a girl, Jean, in 1933 and a boy, Eric, the following year. At fifty-one, the Mayor was the foster father of very young children and had known married life for a total of only seven years.

In the nearly three decades he had lived in New York Fiorello acquired few personal friends, but rather many admirers, acquaintances, colleagues, allies, patrons, protégés, and advisers. He was too competitive to get along intimately with his equals. Only with children could he give himself completely. Hobbies he had none, other than a fondness for classical music. He was as mayor to surround himself with more intellectuals than any of his predecessors, but he had either no time or no taste for literature, not even for biography and history, and rarely read anything not directly relevant to his work.[20] He had lived, and would continue to live, mostly for his career and, what is equally important, for the affectionate acclaim that his public personality generated in a vast but impersonal audience. New York had in 1934 a full-time mayor.

La Guardia brought other qualities to the mayoralty in addition to his hybridism, his ambition, and his compassion for the oppressed. There was his gusto for work and his slashing wit, his quick but retentive mind and his theatrical flair. He also brought a considerable experience, stretching back to 1901 when he received his commission as consul agent from John Hay, Secretary of State under the first Roosevelt. By 1934 La Guardia had spent all but six years of his majority in one Government job or another. Public service was a way of life for him.

He clearly qualified for the office sometimes described as second in difficulty only to the Presidency as an elective office in American government. And by the late 1930's Republicans of the stature of William Allen White were booming him for the Presidency itself. Twelve years after his death in 1947, Professor Rexford G. Tugwell saluted him as "a great man in the Republic" and, excepting only F.D.R. among his contemporaries, as "the best-known leader in our democracy. . . ."[21] Many people today accept that estimate as valid.

But the historian cannot stop there.

3. *A Near Miss*

The historian cannot stop there because La Guardia's career before he became mayor fell far short of greatness. He had been a good and even important consul agent, interpreter, deputy state attorney general, Army officer, president of the Board of Aldermen, and Congressman—but people of that sort, no matter how good and important, are hardly the sort whom the history books celebrate. La Guardia's renown dates from the mayoralty years, and we must therefore ask why a man of his obvious talent and ambition failed, except for the Norris–La Guardia Act of 1932, to make a major impression on American politics before then.

The answer lies in social forces beyond La Guardia's control, but also in serious defects of personality and character.

When he ran unsuccessfully for mayor in 1929, he faced a popular idol in Jimmy Walker, a fabulous machine given a respectable face by Al Smith, and Democratic registrations that outnumbered the Republican by better than three to one. The economy, moreover, was still prosperous. As for the positions La Guardia had won, none of them permitted him to make decisions of real consequence or to carry them out. Even when he held the balance of power in the 1932 Congress as the leader of a small band of progressives, he was more effective in blocking or modifying legislation than in pushing through his own bills, again excepting the Norris–La Guardia Act. Institutions had been beyond his control.

The times had been equally beyond his control. No one during the 1920's opposed more strenuously than Congressman La Guardia prohibition, privileged business, Yankee imperialism, and the Nordic nonsense that led to immigration restriction, or had worked so hard to enlarge the welfare functions of the Federal Government. One New York tabloid called La Guardia "America's Most Liberal Congressman." Yet the complacency and conservatism that dominated the nation's capital was too strong to overcome. Dissenter, critic, and gadfly—a fighter against his times—La Guardia said of himself during the Coolidge years:

"I am doomed to live in a hopeless minority for most of my legislative days."[22]

That was a strange thing for a man to say who had started his career as a loyal Republican in 1910 and whose party controlled both the Congress and the Presidency during the 1920's. But by the latter decade La Guardia was so contemptuous of the moribund New York City organization and so hostile to the Old Guard leadership on the national level that he was a Republican only in name. In East Harlem, where his personal popularity and personal machine were stronger than any party label, he was sometimes in and sometimes out of the G.O.P., usually running for office with the endorsement of other parties in addition to the Republican. "I would rather be right than regular," he said in 1924.[23]

His moralism was as genuine as it was courageous, but the hard fact was, and still is, that the big prizes in Amercian politics usually fall to the men who play the game according to the rules of the two-party system. Except for unusual circumstances, *i.e.*, New York City during the Depression and World War II, irregulars, insurgents, come-outers, bolters, and loners win only the contest for the minds of posterity—if they win even then. Congressman La Guardia lived in a hopeless minority not just because of his times, but also because his personal style unsuited him for the two-party system.

The unattractive features of that style gave the impression that Fiorello was erratic and unstable and therefore unreliable. His party infidelity, cockiness, truculence, irascibility, and demagoguery, not to mention his violent temper, played into the hands of enemies who wanted the public to believe that he *was* a crazy little wop. Men who disagreed with Fiorello were not merely wrong; he denounced them as betrayers of the public trust. Yet he himself was not unfree from lapses in disinterested high-mindedness. When a number of Congressmen in 1926 condemned Mussolini as a murderous dictator, La Guardia, although privately loathing Italian Fascism, protested against the condemnation for fear of losing his seat from Latin East Harlem.[24] Those and other defects, particularly visible in a man with a naked ambition for high office, had caused New Yorkers of nearly every political persuasion to doubt, at one time or another in his career, that La Guardia was fit to govern the biggest city in America.

That was the sentiment of an *ad hoc* committee of reformers and Republicans that had been formed in the spring of 1933 to select a candidate for mayor to head an anti-machine ticket in the coming fall election. La Guardia wanted desperately to be their choice. The Seabury investigations of Tammany Hall had made New York ripe for a reform movement, and only through the mayoralty could La Guardia rescue a political career that his unexpected defeat for re-election to Congress the previous year had left dangling in the balance. But the committee bypassed him, offering the nomination to a number of men who declined it and finally designating a General John F. O'Ryan to make the race.

La Guardia ultimately made the race, not O'Ryan, and in retrospect one can agree that he was the logical one to do so.

But no one even vaguely familiar with American election politics can think that logic is the sole arbiter of conflict. Because politics is men leading other men, it is subject to the worst as well as to the best in human nature, not to speak of the caprice of chance, timing, accident, and just plain luck. And because politics can take place only in society, it is intertwined with social custom, tradition, habit, and institutions. The complexity and range of variables were such that historians can never fully know how La Guardia in 1933 came to be thought of as the right man for the right job at the right time, but the answer as to why he came to be thought so lies not only in himself but in the New Yorkers and the New York that grudgingly gave him his prize.

II

The Little Flower and the Mayflower

There is no single path to the mayoralty in America, for no city is quite like another. The sudden and sprawling expansion of Los Angeles prepared the ground for a faceless newcomer like Samuel Yorty, whereas in Boston an historic Irish-Yankee antagonism paved the way for a tribal chieftain like James Michael Curley. In La Guardia's New York, as a result of a more than half-century-old conflict between machine politicians and reformers, two approaches had been carved out of the political landscape leading to City Hall.

The first lay through the Democratic Party. It was the main-traveled road, for the Democrats had held the mayoralty for all but ten years during the eight and a half decades since the founding of modern Tammany in the 1850's. The second lay through a temporary anti-Tammany coalition known as Fusion and opened up only after an investigation had covered the ruling machine with scandal. It was that route, often attempted but successfully traversed only four times since the Civil War, that La Guardia took in 1933.

But if the result was a traditional victory for reform over a classical big-city machine under the usual conditions, the candidate was wholly unlike any in the past. La Guardia was the first Fusion mayor to be a professional politician, the first to be an Italo-American, and the first not to be what an older generation of mugwumps called a gentleman. His unprecedented triple first smashed a tradition established in the 1872 uprising against the Tweed Ring and thereafter honored at least once a decade for the next fifty years. Fusion mayors had been men of northern European stock who belonged to Gotham's social, professional, or business elite, if not to Society itself.

It would be in the American vein of celebrating the self-made man to give La Guardia sole credit for triumphing over a stuffy custom. But the fact is that it took a brahmin of brahmins, Judge Samuel Seabury, to force the reform gentry to go outside their own class for a mayoralty candidate of the Little Flower's background. Seabury's immense power and prestige derived from the three investigations of New York City's government that bear his name. Conducted between 1930 and 1932 amidst publicity from one end of the country to the other, they were the most spectacular invasion of Tammany's secret life since the Reverend Charles H. Parkhurst in the 1890's, disguised in black-and-white checkered pants and a flowing red flannel tie, had raided the Tenderloin's brothels (the naked ladies of pleasure played leapfrog in the parson's presence) to expose the misalliance between the boss and the madam.

Seldom in American politics has one leader owed so much to another, and we must therefore pause in our narrative of La Guardia's life in order to consider Seabury the man, the Seabury investigations, and Seabury's crucial role in reversing the Fusion nomination in Fiorello's favor when the latter had already given up all hope and his enemies were rejoicing that the designation of General O'Ryan had put an end, once and for all, to an obnoxious career propelled by unstable and dangerous ambitions.

1. A Patrician with a Difference

Nine years older than La Guardia, Seabury was born on Washington's Birthday, 1873, on West Fourteenth Street between Sixth and Seventh Avenues. A direct descendant of the fabled Mayflower couple, John and Priscilla Alden, Seabury came of mixed Yankee-Yorker stock. The Seaburys and the families to which they were united through marriage had been prominent in seventeenth-century New England and there-after in New York as doctors, lawyers, professors, and above all as clergymen. One of Seabury's ancestors, Samuel Jones, was a founder of the New York Bar. Seabury's father, grand-father, great grandfather, great-great grandfather, and great-great-great grandfather had graced the Episcopal pulpit. The best-known of his clerical forebears, great-great grandfather Samuel Seabury, was the first bishop of the Protestant Episco-pal Church in America and, incidentally, a Tory during the Revolution.

The contrast between Seabury's lineage and bearing ("I will not be exceeded in courtesy," he once said) and La Guardia's descent and style was so sharp that the two men gave the appearance of being stock figures in the cast of New York characters. But the contrast was more superficial than actual. The Mayflower descendant was a very special kind of patri-cian, just as the Little Flower was a very uncommon common man, and their divergence from social type led ultimately to their political convergence.

Raised in genteel poverty in a comfortable but plain house on Chelsea Square, Seabury grew to manhood as antagonistic as did La Guardia to what they both called special privilege. Unlike the scions of other first families, Seabury didn't go to Columbia, Harvard, Yale, or some other such institution fa-vored by the New York gentry. The fact is, Seabury's father couldn't afford to send him to college at all. Rector of an Episcopal church in a decaying neighborhood and later a pro-fessor of canon law at General Theological Seminary, the elder Seabury educated his son at home, then enrolled him in a private secondary school, and ran out of money when the boy reached college age. Like La Guardia, Seabury worked his way through law school, opened his own office instead of join-ing an established firm, and plunged immediately into politics as a progressive reformer.[1]

That was back in the 1890's when Lord Bryce remarked that the government of big cities was the most conspicuous failure in American life. His observation applied with particular force to Seabury's New York. There was the failure to cope with the appalling poverty described by Jacob Riis in *How the Other Half Lives*. There was the failure to check the violence and crime and vice against which the Reverend Dr. Parkhurst was thundering from his Madison Square Presbyterian pulpit. There was the failure to remove the sources of political corruption exposed by State Senator Lexow, Lincoln Steffens, Joseph Pulitzer, William Randolph Hearst, and a host of other muckrakers. And there was the failure of nerve of the old families, most of whom shrank from a politics dominated by coarse men of low appetites and improper pedigrees.

The municipal government was controlled, as it had been for decades, by the New York County Democratic Executive Committee. Headed by Richard Croker, who had started life as an unskilled worker (and chief brawler) on the Fourth Avenue tunnel, the committee included one convicted murderer, three ex-prizefighters, four professional gamblers, and half a dozen veterans of the Tweed Ring. Tammany's Republican counterparts, led by Thomas Collier Platt, differed only in their non-Celtic origins. The managers of both major parties ignored social problems, ridiculed reform as so much "gush," dismissed issues as irrelevant to politics, and frankly admitted that they were working for their own pockets all the time.

Just how much loot was made from the sale of franchises, the protection of whorehouses, and other forms of graft is past discovery. It is perhaps enough to say that Croker was exceptional neither in becoming a millionaire through his connections nor in claiming his right to do so before an investigating committee. Politics was a business, like any other, and the business of business was private gain. When Croker was asked for his opinion of free silver, the most controversial political issue of the 1890's, he merely growled: "I'm in favor of all kinds of money—the more the better."[2]

It was in that kind of New York that Seabury cut his first political teeth. He belonged to a gifted generation of gentlemen in politics who, unlike most of their class, joined battle against the cynical spoilsmen and robber barons in order to restore traditional standards of morality to public life. Their methods differed, as did their ultimate objectives, although their activities sometimes crisscrossed. A few, like the Republicans Theodore Roosevelt, Elihu Root, and Henry L. Stimson, joined a district club as a first step toward taking their party away from the crooked bosses so that they could administer the social order as enlightened conservatives. A larger number, among them C. C. Burlingham, William Jay Schieffelin, Richard Welling, Fulton Cutting, and Preble Tucker, founded one association or another to serve as a civic watchdog and promote Fusion. Seabury, although active in the Good Government Clubs and the Citizens Union, was exceptional among his class in proposing the reconstruction of society according to what were then considered radical principles.[3]

For the young patrician brought to politics not only a family and Protestant and class tradition that placed the highest value on disinterested public service, but also a social concern sharpened by early personal struggles. A chance reading of *Progress and Poverty* gave direction to that concern. Seabury devoured Henry George's writings, talked long hours with the author in the latter's Brooklyn home, campaigned like a lay evangelist for him in the 1897 mayoralty contest, and was devastated by his sudden death just before the end of the campaign. The twenty-four-year-old youth was then president of the Single Tax Club of Manhattan, and La Guardia had yet to be graduated from grade school in Arizona.

Years later Seabury remarked that the most important lesson he learned from his mentor was the principle of unselfish leadership. But Henry George was a social engineer, not a Goo Goo, the professional politicians' derisive term for the good government reformer whose aim was merely to throw the rascals out of office and replace them with men of the "better sort." It was more important, Seabury was taught by his mentor, to go after the causes of the Social Problem. He subscribed to the whole of George's program to wipe out poverty, eliminate monopoly, and purify government: a confiscatory tax on unearned landed income, the public ownership of "natural monopolies" (public utilities), and the substitution of

issues for the struggle between rival machines over the patronage and boodle that passed for politics.

Yet despite those ultimate objectives, Seabury was eclectic
in his affiliations. The sort who was willing to accept reform
piecemeal, he supported nearly every movement that promised
to promote social justice, curb big business, or reconstitute the
governing classes. A Bryan and Wilson Democrat in national
affiliation but locally at war with the Croker (later the
Murphy) machine, he was active in the successful Fusion
campaigns for William L. Strong in 1895, Seth Low in 1901,
and John P. Mitchel in 1913, and ran for office with the
support of such groups as the Citizens Union, the Independent
Labor Party, and the Municipal Ownership League.

But Seabury was essentially an independent Democrat, and
by World War I he had proved to be one of the best vote-
getters of that breed in the Empire State. He was elected to
the City Court at twenty-eight, to the State Supreme Court at
thirty-three, and to the august Court of Appeals (the state's
highest tribunal) at forty-one. A moralist in politics, he also
possessed a quality that Disraeli called an instinct for butchery,
which is to say that he welcomed electoral combat because he
enjoyed annihilating an opponent in the name of a cause. In
1916 Theodore Roosevelt, whose Progressive Party two years
earlier had joined reform Democrats in nominating Seabury to
the Court of Appeals, persuaded the Judge to resign from the
bench and run for governor.

"You may assuredly count upon it," Roosevelt told Seabury in promising Progressive backing. "I never will give my
support to Whitman," the Old Guard incumbent.[4]

Seabury won the Democratic nomination and as in 1914
campaigned strongly with the liberal elements of his party.
"He is one of the original leaders of that new American
democracy which is more concerned with human rights than
property," Joseph Pulitzer's *World* wrote approvingly. The
New York City machine, however, sat out the election. Seabury was urging the re-election of President Woodrow Wilson, and Wilson's denunciation of hyphenate Americans (the
Judge took no part in the denunciation) had alienated the
traditional Tammany Irish- and German-American vote. The

powerful Democratic Hearst press also came out against Seabury—previously associated with one another in the Municipal Ownership League, the two men had had a falling out. But the most disturbing and ultimately most serious opposition issued from an unexpected source. Theodore Roosevelt, in a sudden about-face, rejoined the G.O.P. and not only assailed the man he had promised to support but commanded the remnants of the New York State Progressive Party to endorse the re-election of Governor Charles S. Whitman.

There is no telling how far Seabury would have gone in American politics had he entered the Executive Mansion in Albany (a fellow Democrat, Al Smith, was to occupy it two years later). But the Judge lost the election and his defeat embittered him so that he retired to private life, with grudges against Roosevelt, Tammany, Hearst, and Whitman. His final words with T.R., at a tongue-lashing session after the 1916 election in the Rough Rider's Oyster Bay home, were:

"Mr. President, you are a blatherskite!"[5]

Meanwhile, in that same 1916 election, an obscure deputy state attorney general in the Whitman administration was winning his first election to Congress, largely by exploiting the hyphenate vote that had undone Seabury. Not yet the reformer he later would be, the Republican La Guardia demanded a sterner loyalty to the machine than even its leaders were prepared to give. In the 1913 municipal campaign, for example, the Little Flower, then a G.O.P. election district captain in the Italian section of Greenwich Village, not only refused to rally to John P. Mitchel, an independent Democrat, but actually berated his party for joining the Fusion movement behind Mitchel.[6] Seabury, not La Guardia, was more right than regular during the Progressive Era.

Then, in a change of roles during the 1920's, the East Harlem insurgent articulated a new progressivism stemming from the slums, while Tory Bishop Samuel Seabury's great-great grandson seemed to revert to type.

He earned big money as a lawyer, making a million dollars alone in settling the Jay Gould legacy, and bought a Central Park East mansion and enlarged a modest summer retreat into a Long Island estate. The life he led prompted observers to

remark that he was the closest specimen to an English gentleman on this side of the Atlantic. He conducted his law
practice like a London barrister and dressed like a landed
squire during weekend retreats in the country. Summer vacations he spent in Britain, which he adored, tracing the family
tree and collecting rare books, prints, and paintings for his
magnificent Tudor-style library (two stories high, sixty feet
long, forty feet wide) in East Hampton. Seldom during the
1920's did he raise his voice in public on the issues of the
day.

When Seabury suddenly swooped out of the past to take on
Tammany Hall in 1930, it was hard to believe that he had
voted for Populist Tom Watson in the 1904 Presidential election or that he had once been a municipal socialist or a scrappy
stump orator in a dozen and more brutal political campaigns. It
was easier to think of him as simply being a very rich man
with an illustrious genealogy and a formidable dignity. Ruddy-
faced and white-haired, wearing pince-nez and carrying a
cane, his tall and portly and middle-aged body clothed by
English tailors, he inspired journalists to outdo themselves in
portraying him as the bluest of blue bloods.

"Judge Seabury is perhaps the most thoroughly patrician
figure in our public life today—at a period when any hint of
aristocracy is supposed to be fatal," the *Literary Digest* commented with awe in 1933.[7]

That was how La Guardia felt in the spring of that year
when he and Seabury met for the first time. The Little Flower
did not immediately win him over his candidacy, as we shall
later see, but the Judge was not prejudiced against him. Too
secure to be a snob, Seabury had also been around long enough
to know that gentlemen could be blatherskites and that a
former judicial colleague by the name of Cardozo, even
though the son of a Tweed henchman, could give lessons in
ethics to a Roosevelt. Conduct was still his sole test of excel-
lence.

Notwithstanding a recent affluence and a newly-acquired
passion for things English, Seabury was still a patrician with a
difference. Less radical than thirty years before, he nevertheless had escaped the conservatism that overcomes some reformers with advancing years. If no longer a single taxer, he

had remained a liberal enough Democrat during his retirement to approve of Al Smith's Presidential ambitions. And if he had outgrown a youthful certainty in the wisdom of socializing *all* public utilities, he would be a chief negotiator for Mayor La Guardia in the acquisition of a municipal subway system. He still had plenty of reform zeal and was to expend it on a cause in which his faith had never flagged; namely, that New York City deserved a more responsible governing class than semi-literate clubhouse politicians who confused private gain with the public good.

Unknowingly and indirectly, La Guardia contributed to the circumstances resulting in Seabury's return to politics and, therefore, in their ultimate alliance against Tammany Hall.

When La Guardia ran for mayor in 1929 he accused Tammany of having links to the underworld. The principal evidence he offered came in the form of a sensational disclosure that Magistrate Albert H. Vitale of the Bronx, who was getting out the Italian vote for Tammany, had received a loan of nearly $20,000 from the murdered gangster Arnold Rothstein. "There isn't a Tammany politician that would dare to have his bank account examined,"[8] Fiorello charged. He appealed to Albany to investigate the downstate Democratic machine, but Governor Franklin D. Roosevelt ruled that not enough facts had been presented to warrant such an inquest.

One month after the 1929 election, however, Vitale was sitting down to a political dinner in his honor at a Democratic clubhouse when masked gunmen burst into the room and staged a holdup. Among the notables seated at the festive board were half a dozen or so hoodlums, the most notorious of them being Ciro Terranova, who was known by the engaging sobriquet, King of the Artichoke Racket. Why the holdup took place still remains a mystery, but a few hours later Vitale arranged to have the stolen items returned, including the service revolver of a detective who had been one of the diners! The magistrate's achievement raised embarrassing questions about his connections, and the Bar Association inquired into his affairs, discovering that La Guardia had been dead right about that Rothstein loan.

On March 14, 1930, Judge Vitale was no longer a judge.

Meanwhile, scandals involving other Democratic appointees

to the bench broke into the headlines, and La Guardia joined
in a city-wide cry for a judicial housecleaning. Governor
Roosevelt then asked the Appellate Division of the Supreme
Court to exercise its authority to investigate the Magistrates'
Courts.* The Appellate Division voted to do so on August 26,
1930, and chose Seabury, a former colleague and a judge's
judge and a lawyer's lawyer, as referee.[9]

Seabury received the news of his appointment in a London
hotel while he was browsing through a first (1631) edition of a
rare book, *The Just Lawyer*, which he had just tracked down
to add to his large collection in legal history. Bored with
private life, he accepted the assignment immediately and set
sail for America. At almost the same moment Mayor Jimmy
Walker was in a Long Island restaurant with his mistress
trying to avoid arrest in a sudden gambling raid.[10] Two years
later, after the original investigation of the courts had widened
to include the whole of New York City's government,† the
indefatigable Judge was to face the playboy Mayor in the
climactic scene of a public show that a nation-wide audience
had been watching with a mixture of disbelief, hilarity, and
disgust.

2. *The Machine, the Boss, and Tammany Hall*

Some four thousand witnesses appeared in private and public
hearings and their testimony filled nearly ninety-five thousand
pages of transcript. Seabury could not indict, try, or convict

---

* These were the courts that New Yorkers, if they went to court, were
most familiar with. There were some fifty of them, one for each
district to transact general criminal business, and five special courts for
cases involving homicide, commercial frauds, domestic disputes, traffic
violations, and delinquent women. Seabury had authority to examine
the courts only in Manhattan and the Bronx.

† On March 28, 1931, while Seabury was still inquiring into the Magistrates' Courts, Governor Roosevelt appointed Seabury to examine charges
filed against Manhattan's aged and allegedly incompetent district attorney, Thomas T. C. Crain. On April 8 of the same year, the Joint
Legislative Committee to Investigate the Affairs of the City of New
York (also called the Hofstadter Committee because that was the name
of its chairman), which had been created by the Republican state
legislature, selected Seabury as counsel. Seabury dominated all three
investigations, which went on simultaneously, so that they became known
by his name.

any of them. Authorized only to ascertain the facts of mal-
feasance, misfeasance and nonfeasance, his strategy was to
bury a rascally breed of politicians under a mountain of muck.

His young staff—many of them only a few years out of law
school and having political ambitions as well as a sincere desire
to clean up the town—performed feats of research for him.
They uncovered evidence having to do with gambling and
prostitution, with influence-peddling, rigged nominations, and
scandalous appointments, with bank books and canceled check
stubs, with letters of credit, brokerage accounts, and safety
deposit boxes: evidence, in short, having to do with municipal
chicanery of the more hoggish sort. Seabury interrogated
witnesses about his staff's findings, and the answers suggested
that E. L. Godkin, editor of the *Nation* and New York
Evening Post during the Tweed-Kelly-Croker regimes, may
well have said the last word on the subject when he remarked:

"The three things a Tammany leader most dreaded were, in
the order of ascending repulsiveness, the penitentiary, honest
industry, and biography."[11]

But Seabury was less interested in calling attention to warts
on individual faces than in portraying an entire ruling class as
corrupt and incompetent. What is even more important, the
purpose of his biographical muckraking was to launch a movement against the institutions through which that class acquired, retained, and exploited power for selfish ends. Therein
lay the connection between the 1930–1932 inquest and the
1933 election. La Guardia did not merely campaign against
Tammany, he promised to destroy the system of bosses and
machines and to replace it with nonpartisan government by
experts. Only then could New York City cope with the
genuine needs of its people.

That was a radical program, striking at structures and
processes and styles in politics as old as political democracy in
American cities. Seabury and La Guardia were proposing to
do away with government by political parties on the municipal
level. The point needs to be emphasized, because the rhetoric
of good intentions has obscured it. In the lexicon of big-city
reform, which dates from the mugwump entries of the late
nineteenth century, the *machine* has been a pejorative term for

the party organization, the *boss* an epithet for the leader of that organization, and *Tammany* an invective for the Democratic organization of New York City.

The organization, party leadership, Tammany—a word is in order about the origins and functions and evolutions of each before turning to why the La Guardia–Seabury generation linked the three institutions as an unholy trinity and condemned them as a blight, a curse, and an excrescence on the body politic, a cancer that had to be removed lest democracy perish.

The Society of Saint Tammany, named for a legendary Delaware Indian chief, was founded in 1789 for patriotic, charitable, and fraternal purposes. Tradesmen and artisans predominated in the membership and at least one-third were bankers. In the Society they took the ranks of hunter, warrior, or sachem (chief). A Grand Sachem presided with the assistance of a Sagamore and a Wiskinski. The clubhouse was called the Wigwam, months were known as moons, seasons bore pseudo-Indian names, and on national holidays the braves donned feathers and war paint to go whooping through the streets. Tammany, in short, began primarily as a nonpolitical club—with the aims, mumbo-jumbo ritual, and hoopla common to the service organizations that dot the American landscape today.

But over the years it came to be the club to which the leading Democrats of the city belonged. By the middle of the nineteenth century Tammany was to the Democratic Party what the Union League Club would be to the Republican Party during and after the Civil War. In 1854 Fernando Wood became the first Tammany Democrat Mayor of New York City. An even better symbol of the merger that had taken place was the election in 1860 of William Marcy Tweed as chairman of the Democratic Party's central committee for New York County and in 1863 as Grand Sachem of Tammany. This was the same "Boss" Tweed whose infamous ring looted the city and who died in disgrace in Ludlow Street Jail.

By the time of the Seabury investigations, membership in Tammany and leadership in the Democratic organization had been so parallel over such a long period of time that the Wigwam had become Gotham's doge's palace. Yet the organization had its own structure, ranks, ceremonies, and activities. Its beginnings dated from the creation of popularly supported political parties after the extension of the franchise to all white adult men in the 1820's and the arrival of huge numbers of immigrants during the second quarter of the nineteenth century. Until then the gentry had governed the city. They were overrun, routed, and displaced by new men like Tweed and Wood who were closer in background than the scions of old families to the mass of recent voters.*

To capitalize on that vote, party managers perfected the rudimentary machinery that previously had existed. The process went on in all parties, but the Democrats exploited the electorate more artfully than the nativist-tinged Whigs and the Republicans who later succeeded the Whigs. By the 1850's an elaborate apparatus of committees reached into virtually every neighborhood of the city. Already the sons of Irish immigrants were conspicuous as leaders, but not until John Kelly's succession to Tweed's chairmanship a decade after the Civil War did the era of Celtic hegemony begin. The Irish then were the largest and also the most self-conscious ethnic group in town.

By 1930, having grown to thirty-two thousand committeemen, the Democratic organization was triple the size of New York City's entire population after the Revolution. But its strength was due not merely to its awesome numbers. The men who ran the organization were on the job day in and day out and knew the voters in their districts. To stay in power, George Washington Plunkitt said, "Study human nature and act accordin'." What is equally important, the leaders were loyal to and accepted the discipline of the hierarchy of which

* Wood was born in Philadelphia and "reached the mayoral chair from beginnings so small," Lord Bryce has written, "that he was . . . reported to have entered New York as the leg of an artificial elephant in a travelling show." *The American Commonwealth* (New York, 1907), II, 382. Tweed was the son of a Scots immigrant and was originally a chairmaker's apprentice. His successors as New York County Democratic chairmen also had working-class backgrounds and immigrant parents. John Kelly started out as a soapstone cutter, Richard Croker as an unskilled laborer, Charles F. Murphy as a horse-car driver, and John F. Curry as a messenger boy.

they were proud parts. "Have you seen Croker?" one party manager asked another who had just announced that he was planning to be married.

New York City's five counties were divided into assembly districts that were in turn subdivided into election districts. On each of the three levels party affairs were managed by a "boss" assisted by a committee. The organization was huge because, by the 1930's, New York City contained close to four thousand election districts and sixty-two assembly districts (twenty-three each in Manhattan and Brooklyn, eight in the Bronx, six in Queens, and two in Staten Island). A chain of command held the structure together. The election district captain was subordinate to his assembly district leader who for his own part owed obedience to his county chairman.

Beginning with the formidable Charles F. Murphy, who reigned from 1902 to 1924, the Manhattan chairman claimed to speak for the whole New York City Democratic organization. That was also the ambition of John F. Curry, chairman of Manhattan since 1929. But Curry, a dour, hardworking, middle-aged district leader who had fought his way up through the West Side slums, possessed only a fraction of his powerful predecessor's ability. He ruled in conjunction with the chairmen of the three other populous counties: John H. McCooey of Brooklyn, John Theofel of Queens, and Edward J. Flynn of the Bronx. An oddity among his fellows, Flynn was a college graduate (Fordham), a loyal supporter of Franklin Roosevelt, and the only one of the big four to emerge unscathed from the Seabury investigations.

The functions of the organization, like those of political parties in general, were to select candidates for appointive and elective office, draw up a platform, get out the vote, and if victorious to govern for all the people. Neither La Guardia nor Seabury denied the necessity of someone to perform those services in a representative democracy. The big question raised by the Seabury investigations was whether the Democratic Party leaders—or the bosses of the Tammany machine—had fulfilled their duties honestly, efficiently, and in the public interest.[12]

Let's look at the record, if we may borrow a phrase from the most famous sachem of the Hall.

3. *A Monumental Muckrake*

Unable to interrogate all thirty-two thousand Democratic committeemen or to investigate their influence on all the nearly 150,000 municipal employees, Seabury concentrated on the bigger fry, hoping to demonstrate that it was in the nature of the machine to produce a derelict mayor, a shockingly bad judiciary, and more generally a government staffed by unqualified men of doubtful honesty.

The example of John Theofel, boss of Queens since 1928, is illustrative.

Born in Manhattan's Slaughter House District, Theofel moved to Queens as a youth, worked briefly as a bus boy, entered politics on the election district level, rose to assembly district leader, and became chairman of the county organization in his late fifties. One of the men he arranged to put in office, the presiding judge of the Surrogate's Court, in turn appointed him chief clerk of that court. The Queens sachem had no legal background and had in fact quit school at an early age like so many other Tammany chieftains.

When Seabury asked him to describe his duties as chief clerk and name the departments under his jurisdiction, Theofel's answer was, "I can't just recall offhand, Judge, the different departments, but I walk around the office and keep them on the job."

"Are your duties arduous?" Seabury further inquired. "How much of your time do they take?"

"Some."

"Some?"

"About nine o'clock to about two o'clock. Maybe later."

"And do you also have a vacation?"

"I took the month of July."

"How about when bleak winter winds blow?"

"I had a vacation in February. Two weeks. I went to Hot Springs."[13]

What strikes one in reading Theofel's testimony was not so much his transparent unfitness to hold the ranking administrative post of an important court but his genuine surprise that Seabury should have raised the question of fitness as a test for public office. The interrogator and the witness used the same words but attached different meanings to them. What did fitness have to do with politics? Politics was jobs and jobs was politics and jobs went to men who served the organization. What other reason was there to work for the party?

Unfortunately, Theofel's remarks on the distribution of patronage are too long to reproduce, for he expressed himself with revealing and guileless candor. The essence of his testimony was that in 1931 the Democratic and Republican county chairmen of the city got together in advance to divide the spoils of twelve additional State Supreme Court justiceships the Albany legislature was just about to create. After much bargaining two of the plums fell to the Queens Democratic machine—"I would like to have gotten the whole twelve if I could,"[14] Theofel explained to Seabury, in order to "meet" the party "situation" in his county—and the bipartisan slate selected by the bosses was nominated and elected.

(One of the new judges from Brooklyn was thirty-one-year-old John H. McCooey, Jr., and Seabury summoned Boss John H. McCooey, Sr., of Brooklyn to the witness stand to explain why his son, no legal prodigy, merited a $25,000 nomination to the bench. "Oh," said the father, "nearly every leader in the party urged me very strongly to nominate Jack. I had no idea there was such a unanimity of opinion." Besides, Jack was not only "in a receptive mood," he had "the poise and the character and the industry. . . .")[15]

Seabury's staff brought to light the fact that Theofel was worth close to a quarter of a million dollars. How did he amass that fortune on a chief clerk's salary of $8,000 a year? The hearings revealed that Theofel owned an automobile agency with his son-in-law and the latter's brother, Wilson Bros., Inc., a firm that did a thriving business in selling both official and private cars to Queens's officeholders. "I wanted to buy a car from another agency, but Dudley Wilson is the son-in-law of Theofel, and it is the usual thing to do as the Boss says," Sheriff Samuel Burden testified.[16]

George Washington Plunkitt, the celebrated sage of Tammany Hall, called that sort of thing *honest graft*. Without stealing from the public till, Theofel could have said as Plunkitt did, "I seen my opportunities and I took 'em." But in another part of his testimony, going back to when he had been treasurer of the Queens Democratic finance committee, Theofel reported that he saw the chairman take $6,000 from the party fund and give it to the secretary.

"I protested," Theofel said indignantly, in recalling the incident for Seabury.

" 'Take a thousand for yourself, John,' the chairman told me."

"Well, did you?" Seabury wanted to know.

"Sure," was the answer.[17]

Theofel's exceptional frankness made him such a good witness for Seabury's purpose that it's hard to imagine how a better one could have been invented. What is more, he was physically so gross, with a huge belly, massive face, rolls of fat under his chin, pouched eyes, and a stupid stare, that reporters delighted in caricaturing him as an authentic Neanderthal. But whatever the size, shape, or temperament of the other bosses, they shared Theofel's view of public office as a form of private property. The city chamberlain, the budget director, the president of the taxes and assessment department, the county sheriffs, clerks of all sort, the fire commissioner, and commissioners of parks, purchase, public buildings, public works, docks—there's no need to go on—these and other heads and subheads of government departments were organization leaders from one county or another. They knew as little about their work as did Theofel about his. Their jobs gave them a title, an office with a staff, a car, and a salary ranging up to $17,500 per annum. And there was additional money, as in Theofel's case, to be made on the side. For example,

—James A. McQuade, Brooklyn's Fifteenth Assembly District coleader and Kings County Register, banked $520,000 in six years.

—James J. McCormick, leader of Manhattan's Twenty-second Assembly District and Deputy City Clerk in charge of marriage ceremonies, deposited $384,788 between 1925 and 1931.

—Thomas M. Farley, Manhattan's Fourteenth Assembly District leader and Sheriff of New York County since 1930, saved $360,660.34 in six-and-a-half years.

—Charles W. Culkin, coleader of Manhattan's Third Assembly District and Farley's predecessor as sheriff, put away $1,929,759 in seven years.[18]

It will probably never be known with any exactitude how much *dishonest* graft filtered into the pockets of these and other leaders. Boodle was not the kind of thing the machine kept a record of. Culkin refused to waive immunity and therefore did not testify in public hearings about the sources of his two-million-dollar bank account. Others pleaded amnesia. Still others invented what Seabury called, in a rare outburst, "a cock and bull story that is just as amazing as they are."[19]

James McCormick estimated that he had made around $150,000 in "tips" from bridegrooms in the performance of his duties as marriage clerk at the Municipal Building during the previous six years, but when asked to account for the remainder of the nearly four hundred thousand dollars he had deposited, he mumbled: "Why, I didn't know I had so much." Indicted for income tax evasion and convicted, he resigned both his city job and district leadership. Thereafter huge signs were posted in the marriage bureau informing couples that they were to pay two dollars to the clerk and no more.

James McQuade insisted that the more than half a million dollars he had banked over the years was "money that I borrowed." His coleader, the famed Peter J. McGuinness, dubbed him "Payroll Jim, The Jesse James of Greenpoint." Short and stocky, with rimless eyeglasses and a fake dignity, McQuade spoke in a torrent of words. The substance of his long and involved testimony was that, after an initial loan, he borrowed from B to pay back A, from C to pay back B, from D to pay back C, and so on through the alphabet, until he found himself possessing some five hundred thousand dollars in 1931!

When asked to name the men he had borrowed from, McQuade replied sadly to Seabury, "I can't offhand, Judge, remember that far back. I had troubles enough. . . ."

After stepping down from the witness stand he turned to

the newspapermen. "You fellows ought to know," he said. "How did my story go over?" McQuade had testified that he had gone into "debt" solely to support "the other thirty-three McQuades," dear relatives all, whom the most awful calamities had left destitute. The New York *Sun* did the Greenpoint leader the unkindness of assigning a reporter to check out his story. Far from being destitute, the thirty-three other Mc-Quades turned out to be prospering in the real estate business or doing very nicely indeed on the public payroll.

What were McQuade and McCormick (and others) hiding? Certain that many a district leader's fortune derived from the protection of professional gambling, Seabury summoned Sheriff Farley as a witness. A police raid on Farley's clubhouse in 1926 had turned up a number of well-known gamblers standing around a crap table. The sheriff, a jolly fat man who enjoyed his day in the box, questioned the accuracy of the police report. He testified that he had arrived at his clubhouse just after the police and that neither the men nor the paraphernalia he saw there had anything to do with crapshooting.

"The members that was there," he recalled, "was busy packing baseball bats, skipping ropes, and rubber balls, because our May Day party took place the next day."

Seabury was unsatisfied. "Well, what else besides baseball bats, rubber balls, and skipping ropes did you find there after the raid?" No crap table?

"There was canopies and May-poles," Farley replied in injured tones.

Well, then, how did the sheriff, who left school at thirteen, manage to deposit nearly $400,000 in six years on a total salary of some $90,000?

"It represented moneys I had saved. I took the money out of a safe-deposit box at home," was Farley's explanation.

"And Sheriff," Seabury asked after a long series of questions establishing the precise size and exact location of that box, "was this big box that was safely kept in the big safe a tin box or a wooden box?"

"A tin box," was the answer.

"Kind of a magic box, wasn't it, Sheriff?"

"It was a wonderful box," the witness agreed.[20]

That's how the Seabury investigations came to be known as the Tin Box Parade. New York City laughed, and so did Farley, until Governor Roosevelt summoned him to Albany. Clad in wing collar and morning coat, the sheriff hoped that perhaps his contribution of $20,000 to a previous Roosevelt campaign would be remembered. The governor removed him from his $15,000-a-year job, ruling that a public official must give "a reasonable or credible explanation" of the difference between one's public salary and one's bank account.

Influence-peddling was perhaps the most lucrative form of loot for the machine. The North German Lloyd Steamship Company paid a $50,000 "fee" to lawyer William H. Hickin, who was also president of the National Democratic Club, to "process" its application for a Hudson River dock. Unwilling to waive immunity, Hickin did not appear before Seabury. The law firm of Olvany, Eisner and Donnelly, Esq., whose senior partner was the Democratic chairman of Manhattan from 1925 to 1929, made a good deal of its more than a million dollars a year from clients who did business with the city. Asked if his political leadership would help his law practice, Olvany replied: "Well, it won't hurt it any."[21]

The biggest grafter of all was perhaps "Doc" (William F.) Doyle, a veterinarian by education, who had been practicing an unorthodox kind of medicine before the Board of Standards and Appeals. The power of the board to vary building and zoning regulations was worth millions of dollars to real estate interests. Doyle won some five hundred cases in the 1920's, banking in 1927 alone $243,692.60 in fees. What was the source of his success? He had no training as engineer, lawyer, builder, or architect.

"Go see the Doctor," the Chairman of the Board advised one innocent man who began to argue a case on its merits.

"But I'm not sick," the man said.

"See the Doctor," he was told again.[22]

When Seabury asked Doyle if he had been splitting his fees, Doyle refused to answer the question on the ground that it might tend to incriminate him. He was cited for contempt and sentenced to jail for thirty days, but Boss Curry phoned a sympathetic judge of the appellate division who was vacationing at Lake Placid to stay the order. Himself summoned to the witness box, Curry cried out to Seabury: "This is a crucifiction, if it can be had, of the Democratic party of the City of New York."[23]

One could go on and on with examples, but they would only prove further Seabury's point that the bosses had debased politics into a questionable way of earning a living (it should be added that for the bosses politics was also a game they enjoyed playing more than any other). Seabury snorted over the alleged difference between "honest" and "dishonest" graft. To hold a job without being qualified for it, to accept tips from bridegrooms, to peddle cars to the city from one's agency—such activities were no less dishonest for a public official than selling influence to gamblers, steamship lines, and real estate men. Heaven only knows what other opportunities were seen and taken. Not even a ten million dollar relief fund for the unemployed had been safe from plunder.[24]

All this was awful in itself, but Seabury extended his indictment, claiming that a politics based on private gain inevitably resulted in cheating the public out of services it had a right to expect and enjoy from government. More specifically, he traced "the hideous caricature which parades as justice" in the Magistrates' Courts to the district leader system.

"Now, will you tell us a little more," Seabury was questioning Magistrate Maurice Gottlieb of Yorkville, "about the circumstances of your appointment to the bench?"

"Well, I can explain that," Gottlieb said without hesitation. "I have been a member of Tammany Hall over forty years. . . . I helped get the house that our clubhouse is in. I have done things to help build up our organization in our district."[25]

The fifty-odd judges of the city's lower courts held their tenure by virtue of a mayoral appointment usually recommended by their district leader. The head clerks of the court were also appointed, and although assistant clerks and court attendants fell under civil service, the loose merit requirements were no obstacle to rewarding loyal party workers. Twenty-four court officers freely admitted that like Gottlieb they had earned their jobs merely by serving the organization. More important, they were morally certain that that's the way it should be. Some of them scarcely knew the difference between a telephone book and a law book. All of them believed that it was only right and proper for the district leader to intervene in cases. Fixing was therefore as rife in the courts as it was in the Board of Standards and Appeals.

Some of that fixing was vile. Seabury uncovered a ring of bondsmen, lawyers, Vice Squad policemen, court attendants, and an assistant district attorney operating out of the Women's Court who hired *provocateurs* not only to shake down prostitutes, but also to frame innocent women as call girls or madams. Victims who could not or would not raise the cash or bail to buy their freedom went to jail. The racket paid handsomely over the years, but it attracted types for whom money was not the sole motive. A medical report of one innocent woman stated that the arresting police officer had given her a black eye, bruised her thighs and belly, and left signs "above her right breast which resembled teeth marks."[26]

One of the presiding judges, Mrs. Jean H. Norris, a former district leader whose appointment to the bench had been arranged by Charles Murphy in 1919, was ignorant of the ring that functioned in her court. Handing down stiff sentences and giving lectures on virtue in a counterfeit genteel accent, she convicted several guiltless defendants on the testimony of perjurious witnesses. When she discovered her mistake in one case she changed the court record to hide the fact that she had prevented the client's lawyer from making a full defense. Seabury's investigators also brought to light that Her Honor was a stockholder in a surety company that issued bonds she as a judge often approved. Picking up still other side money, she posed in her judge's gown for Fleischmann's Yeast advertisements and was quoted as saying that after trying that product "the improvement in my digestion resulted in more restful sleep than I had had for years."

Seabury demanded Judge Norris's removal by the appellate division and got it.

Not since the Page Commission of the first decade of this century had there been as thorough an exposé of the city's lower criminal courts as Seabury's. The results? Twenty-six persons resigned or were dismissed from the bench, police department, and district attorney's office; six men were tried and convicted for crimes; and the Vice Squad was disbanded. Yet Seabury had aimed toward more lasting consequences. In his final report he recommended sweeping institutional and procedural changes to remove the judiciary from the spoils system, the source of injustice. Some of his proposed reforms were adopted in the years that followed, but even today the mayor appoints magistrates.[27]

4. Duel at Foley Square

The day finally came, May 25, 1932, when Samuel Seabury faced James J. Walker in the jam-packed courtroom of the New York County Courthouse off Foley Square and said firmly but courteously: "Mr. Mayor, would you be good enough to take the stand." The encounter lasted for two days. There were seats for only three hundred and forty-three spectators, and an overflow crowd of six thousand milled in the corridors of the building and the street outside to glimpse the two feature players of the big show. Walker drew the most cheers.

Still youthful at fifty-one and radiating a Broadway breeziness that had made him the toast of the town, Walker was a former songwriter who had given up Tin Pan Alley for politics to please his aging Tammany father. Had he applied his superb native intelligence to City Hall, which he entered in 1925 after fifteen years in the state legislature, he could have been an outstanding mayor. He became instead a playboy who expressed the longings and hopes and values of innumerable New Yorkers in a decade when the heart of the city seemed to beat on the Great White Way. Taking extended vacations on two continents, consorting with celebrities, and carrying on a publicized extramarital love affair, he indulged himself in an endless round of pleasure at theaters, night clubs, speakeasies, restaurants, gambling joints, race tracks, and the like. Wherever he went they said of him, as Toots Shor did, "Jimmy! Jimmy! When you walked into the room you brightened up the joint."[28] In 1929 an adoring electorate returned him to office against La Guardia by a margin just short of a half million.

Meanwhile, the organization took the town, and not even after the Seabury probe began did the mayor think it necessary to scour his administration. On the contrary, with an immense tolerance for human weakness and a genius for the *bon mot*, he met criticisms with witticisms. When asked to justify his elevating former Mayor ("Red Mike") Hylan to the bench of the Children's Court of Queens, the Mayor quipped: "the appointment of Judge Hylan means the children can now be tried by their peer." Some time later he was to remark of Seabury: "This fellow would convict the Twelve Apostles if he could." It was in that spirit that he took the witness stand.

"Little Boy Blue is about to blow his horn—or his top," Walker remarked to his valet before leaving the house for his first appearance against Seabury. The mayor drew up to the courthouse in a blue limousine, waving a hand that flashed a ring with a blue stone, and emerged wearing a single-button double-breasted blue suit, blue tie, blue shirt, and blue pocket handkerchief. He returned to the stand the next day in another blue suit, but with gray accessories that included spats. "Life is just a bowl of Seaburys," he said merrily after the session was over and he was walking back to his car. "Attaboy, Jimmy," the crowd chanted.[29]

He made a mistake in underestimating his adversary. All of Seabury's loathing for Tammany Hall, a hatred he had been nursing for forty years, centered on the dapper little mayor. He didn't merely scorn Walker's personal style as cheap and unbecoming in a chief executive, he intended to destroy the titular head of an administration whose ruling party had debased a city in which he as a patricain felt a proprietary and even patrimonial interest. Curry had been Walker's choice as leader of the Hall.

Walker's testimony was witty and defiant but it was also hollow and unconvincing because it was undocumented and unprepared. He was defenseless as a witness. During the previous year, while he was neglecting his official duties and giving the impression that his most serious problem was the domestication of his beautiful but erratic mistress, the English actress Betty Compton, Seabury's staff had been piecing together the jigsaw puzzle of Walker's personal finances and the chaotic parts of his administration. Confronting the mayor with that record, the Judge reduced him, as Raymond Moley has written, to "evasion, amnesia, cheap theatrics and shallow, unbelievable rationalizations."[30]

Seabury's case against Walker rested mainly on two points. The first of these was that the mayor had accepted approximately three hundred thousand dollars from men who did business with the city or hoped to. The second was that he owned jointly with Russell T. Sherwood, his financial agent, a safe-deposit box in which Sherwood had made deposits totaling nearly one million dollars (of which seven hundred and fifty thousand had been in cash). Not only had Sherwood fled to Mexico to avoid testifying, but Walker had done nothing, at least to public knowledge, to summon his agent back to New York City.

The mayor pleaded innocent to any knowledge of the safe-deposit box in his name and insisted that the three hundred thousand dollars he had received were gifts (he called them "beneficences") from friends. Seabury was certain that Walker had taken bribes, but the evidence for that belief was circumstantial rather than conclusive. In the end it matters little whether the weaknesses of Tammany's Golden Boy included graft. By his own testimony Walker condemned himself as the grossest administrative slob and, if not a crook, as the most shameless freeloader in the history of the New York mayoralty.[31]

Seabury filed charges against the mayor with Governor Roosevelt. Walker had a two-week hearing in Albany, protesting his innocence and disputing the governor's jurisdiction over his tenure, but the precedent established in the case of Sheriff Farley ruled against him. Walker could not credibly explain the difference between his official salary and his personal assets. "Jim, you're through," Al Smith told the man he had tapped to run for mayor in 1925. "You must resign for the good of the party."[32]

Walker did just that, on September 1, 1932, and set sail for

Europe to join Betty Compton. F.D.R., by then the Democratic nominee for President (Seabury had hoped that the lightning would strike himself), was spared a decision that would have antagonized either Democrats for Tammany or voters against the big-city machine.

5. *"So Here's to John Curry"*

"Ernest," said La Guardia to a young admirer when he learned Walker had quit, "this is a great day for our country."[33]

Yet Tammany seemed to have lost nothing but honor. The district leader system was still intact, the tin box brigade was still flourishing, and the Democratic Party was still the most popular one with the New York City electorate. McQuade, the Jesse James of Greenpoint, ran successfully for sheriff of Kings County after testifying before Seabury. More important, in the special election held in November of 1932 to fill Walker's vacancy for one year, the organization nominated a winner in Surrogate John Patrick O'Brien, an old Tammany work horse.

Previously unknown to the public, O'Brien claimed the additional virtue of being unlike his exiled predecessor. Bald and fatherly, earnest and conscientious, as inept at off-the cuff speaking as Walker had been brilliant, O'Brien was a Catholic in good standing, the proud parent of splendid children, and the sort of husband who went home at night to his own wife. He overwhelmed his Republican opponent, Lewis H. Pounds, by a margin of 612,214 votes.

More than a thousand braves from the Manhattan Wigwam gathered at the Hotel Commodore in a victory dinner to celebrate the grand sachem who had decided to run O'Brien. "So Here's to John Curry," they sang to the tune of "In Old Shanty Town,"

> So here's to John Curry,
>   The Chief of the Clan;
> We won't have to worry
>   While he's our head man.

All his loyalty fine
  In our hearts we enshrine.
He's the life of the party
  That gave us O'Brien.
The Tiger is strongest
  When John's in his den,
A man among leaders,
  A prince among men.
So let's all raise a toast to the
  Heavens above
For John Curry, the man we all love.[34]

Brooklyn also rang with defiant merriment. Presented with a copy of a proposed civics textbook based on the Seabury investigations that Professor John Dewey of Columbia University had prepared for the City Affairs Committee, McCooey said: "Why shouldn't the school children have this book? It would prove an inspiration to them to see how the Democratic leaders have succeeded." Not only the contents, but the illustrations as well, were brutally anti-Tammany.

The most irreverent photograph showed McCooey, a fat man with a beet-red face and white walrus mustache, milking a cow whose swollen teats hung obscenely between huge haunches. The caption read: "A jolly family man from Brooklyn who loves milking. He is John H. McCooey, Democratic boss, father of a rising young Supreme Court Judge, and brother of an associate superintendent of schools." McCooey chortled when he spotted himself: "Ho-ho! Just look at that now. I remember that picture very well. I sort of look like William Howard Taft there but he was a larger man." A group scene of the five county elders seated on a couch also moved him to admiration: "Ho-ho! Here's us highbinders, big as life."[35] And so on and on. . . .

Yet if Tammany had cause to laugh, a second look at the 1932 election returns reveals that it also had reason to worry. O'Brien ran 399,061 votes behind President Roosevelt and 475,050 votes behind Governor Herbert H. Lehman. His proportion of the total vote cast, 47 per cent, was 13 per cent less than Walker's 1929 return. Morris Hillquit, O'Brien's

Socialist opponent, received 249,887 votes, a record for his party. And Joseph V. McKee, former president of the Board of Aldermen and acting mayor after Walker's resignation, got 234,372 write-in votes even though he had not been a candidate.[36] Losing tens of thousands of ballots because many persons were unfamiliar with the write-in procedure, his name was misspelled in seventy-eight different ways, from Charles Okee to Edward McKoo.

Clearly, with the regular municipal election of 1933 only one year away, Tammany no longer enjoyed the confidence of the majority. New York City was ripe for Fusion. Two classic conditions favored it: incontrovertible proof of scandal and a split in the Democratic Party. Seabury's monumental muckrake had cost O'Brien between four and five hundred thousand votes. Reform Democrats were feuding with Tammany Democrats, who had refused to ratify Roosevelt's nomination at the Chicago convention, and in September of 1933 a fight between the White House and the Wigwam for control of the local Democracy would tear the organization apart. Two other factors favored reform: the Depression and the New Deal it engendered. Both were making government by semiliterate district leaders obsolete.

Yet O'Brien's easy victory over Pounds had demonstrated that corruption dies hard. To capitalize on their opportunity to throw out a crooked machine, an opportunity that rarely comes to a big city more than once in a generation, anti-Tammany New Yorkers would have to do in 1933 what they had neither the time nor the foresight to do in 1932. They would have to sink their differences in a united front, build a city-wide organization, draft an appealing platform, and nominate for mayor a candidate whose charisma could overcome the massive resignation of the electorate to corruption. Nothing less would bring about a political realignment favoring reform.

La Guardia was as confident that his style of campaigning flashed kindling power as he was that he had earned a first priority on heading an anti-Tammany ticket. Not even the Socialists' Norman Thomas and Morris Hillquit, each of whom had run twice for mayor since World War I, had equaled his persistence in fighting the Hall. On that point the press was unanimous. La Guardia is the only man with the right "to stand up in New York City today and say: 'I told you so,'" the New York *Times* wrote when the Seabury investigation of the Magistrates' Courts was getting under way in 1930. Three years and four thousand witnesses later, that right seemed to be even more indisputable. Who else but La Guardia had "charged Tammany with most of the honeyfuggling," as *Time* put it in the summer of 1933, "which Samuel Seabury later proved in his famed probe"?[37]

III

Nomination After Midnight

La Guardia made his first public gesture toward the mayoralty barely two weeks after his defeat for Congress and O'Brien's election to City Hall. On November 22, 1932, he invited "key men and women in politics and all walks of life to attend" an anti-Tammany meeting in Town Hall on the evening of November 28. Asserting that it was too early to be discussing candidates, he outlined the immediate task to Oswald Garrison Villard of the *Nation* in the following way:

"While everybody is talking about the necessity of a change in our City government, there is nothing really practical, concrete and definite being done. Public opinion must not only be crystallized, but must be translated into action through the medium of an actual fighting organization of determined men and women. The election machinery cannot be overlooked. The best of intentions and good will even of a majority of the people cannot, unless properly prepared, overcome the crookedness, corruption and violence of an entrenched political machine."[1]

During the next three months La Guardia was away from the city, finishing out his term in the lame-duck session of the Seventy-second Congress, where he distinguished himself by introducing legislation for the incoming New Deal administration. Two of his bills, drafted with Professor A. A. Berle, Jr.,

66

of the Roosevelt brain trust, brought the National Bankruptcy Act of 1898 up to date.* These and other constructive measures to save the economy during the worst winter of the Depression kept his name in headlines and reminded New Yorkers that a figure of national stature would soon be available to lead their movement against the discredited Democratic machine.

But when the "Manhattan Messiah" returned home on March 4, 1933, he discovered that machinery to select an anti-Tammany slate of candidates was being set up by civic leaders who wanted no part of him or his kind.

1. *"If It's La Guardia or Bust, I Prefer . . ."*

The Fusion Conference Committee, as it came to be called, consisted of delegates from groups traditionally hostile to the Wigwam: conservative Republicans, the business community, and the Good Government associations. Seldom had those elements favored Fiorello. There were no representatives on the fusionist board of strategy from the press, the clergy, the universities, the bar, the trade unions, the boroughs, or from ethnic groups, women's organizations, social workers, the Socialist Party, the New Deal, or liberal Republicans. The fusionist base was not to be broadened until Seabury's belated but forceful intervention on La Guardia's behalf in midsummer.

Until then La Guardia's ambitions were thwarted by four men (and their occasional assistants) who did the actual work for the Conference Committee. The spokesman for the Republican Party was the same conservative Charles S. Whitman

---

* La Guardia and Berle met for the first time in late 1932 through Paul J. Kern, a La Guardia aide and former student of Professor Berle. The two men took to each other right off. Then a member of F.D.R.'s inner intellectual circle, Berle told Roosevelt that La Guardia belonged on the New Deal train, and Roosevelt agreed that the East Harlem Republican was one of them emotionally and ideologically. When the lame-duck session convened, Berle went to Washington with Roosevelt's permission to get things started as he saw fit. Immediately he had a talk with Vice President-elect John Nance Garner, who was still Speaker of the House, explaining that he wanted La Guardia to introduce legislation for the incoming Administration. Garner told Berle that if anyone could make the "hog wild" Congress do anything it was La Guardia, "a good little wop." For these and further details, see *La Guardia, A Fighter Against His times*, 323–326.

who had defeated Seabury for governor nearly twenty years before. Their feud was to flare up again. The business representative was J. Barstow Smull of the New York State Chamber of Commerce. A steamship broker, his political experience had been limited to serving in the Harding Administration as president of the United States Shipping Board Emergency Fleet Corporation. The other two men were Goo Goos. Joseph M. Price, chairman of the City Club but speaking in the Conference Committee for an *ad hoc* citizens group formed in February of 1933, was a wealthy manufacturer who had been prominent in the Fusion movements of 1913 and 1921 (in the latter year he headed a committee supporting Fiorello's rival in the Republican primary). The fourth man, Maurice P. Davidson of the recently created City Fusion* Party, was a lawyer by trade and had long been active in civic affairs through the Citizens Union.[2]

The City Fusion Party was founded by Davidson and other officers of the Good Government associations immediately after O'Brien's victory in 1932. It grew out of a previous organization, the Committee of One Thousand, which William Jay Schieffelin, chairman of the Citizens Union, had called into being in March of 1931 to pressure the state legislature into investigating the Walker administration. Inspired by the triumph of Cincinnati's Charter Party over the Hynicka machine in the mid-twenties, the City Fusion Party hoped to win the 1933 election and institute such traditional mugwump planks as charter revision, civil service reform, proportional representation, a small city council, possibly a city manager plan, and the consolidation of overlapping offices on which the spoilsmen had been feeding.[3]

Not only did La Guardia stand for much the same things, he had actually been advocating them for a decade and more. His trouble was that he was personally objectionable to the members of the Fusion Conference Committee and, what is equally important, to much of the New York City for which the committee spoke. That New York was educated at the best

* Originally called the City Party, it was renamed in 1933 after it agreed to "fuse" (run a joint ticket) with the Republicans in the campaign of that year.

colleges, financially secure, eminent in the professions and business, and primarily old-stock American Protestant but also significantly Jewish and to a lesser degree Irish-Catholic. The fusionists came, in short, from Gotham's gentry.

The conservative Republicans among them, according to Ed Corsi of East Harlem, despised his friend as "Half Wop, Half American, Half Republican."[4] That Fiorello was the object of out and out prejudice is undeniable. Yet his upper-middle-class antagonists were as a whole parochial rather than bigoted. Like most New Yorkers, they preferred one of their own kind as mayor or at least a type more like themselves than the Italo-American spitfire.

"I want to defeat Tammany," wrote one member of the gentry to another, but "I feel as I did in the beginning that a crude, brawling, loud-mouthed person like La Guardia is the surest way to defeat that end."[5]

La Guardia had been up against that sort of thing before. In 1929, after the Koenig machine had endorsed him because no other serious G.O.P. contender dared to take on the then fabulously popular Jimmy Walker, the Republican press and the party's financial angels rebelled against his candidacy and abused Koenig for nominating him. Some silk-stocking voters actually declared for Norman Thomas, who was at least a gentleman with a Princeton degree even if a Socialist. As for the Goo Goos in 1929, the official publication of Schieffelin's and Davidson's Citizens Union denounced the Little Flower, largely on the basis of his performance as president of the Board of Aldermen (1920–1922), as vulgar and self-seeking, contentious and opportunistic, addicted to "cheap clap-trap and blatant demagogy that passed for declarations of policy. . . ."[6]

Although not without point, such criticism completely overlooked the constructive good that the ungenteel aldermanic president had accomplished in the otherwise disgracefully shoddy Hylan administration. La Guardia therefore had cause to resent being caricatured as a destructive engine of noise. "Nothing hurt me more in 1929 than the unjustifiable attack made on me by the Union," he wrote to an admirer four years later.[7]

Despite all his boasting in private about outdemagoguing the demagogues and inventing the low blow, La Guardia wanted to be known as a responsible and reasonable political leader who fought hard because he fought for worthy causes. Even the slightest insinuation to the contrary—that he brawled for the love of brawling or that he inflamed the crowd for personal advancement—upset him. In 1931, to cite still another example, he took offense at a remark that Lewis Gannett of the *Herald Tribune* made in the course of reviewing a new biography of Richard Croker—namely, "that when the reformers name a roughneck, like Mr. La Guardia, to oppose Tammany, the moneybags are conspicuously lacking."

"Now will you please be good enough to tell me," La Guardia wrote immediately to Gannett, "your definition of a 'roughneck.' Do you really know anything about me, my platform or my policies? Are you familiar with the conditions I had to contend with in the 1929 campaign? I cannot make out if you were trying to be sympathetic or just nasty. Won't you please tell me?"

Gannett, reminding La Guardia that they had met when he had worked for the *Nation* before joining the *Herald Tribune,* assured the Congressman that he was sympathetic. "I like you," he replied. "I like roughnecks. I hope you will not plead that you are not a roughneck. If you do, I shall lose faith in you." Gannett was not being condescending. "I don't think reform politics in New York will ever get anywhere," he continued, "until it gets away from the people who were born with frock coats on their backs and silk hats on their heads. The point of my remark was meant to be a criticism of the moneybags who did not give you as ardent financial support as they would have given to a much less colorful and able candidate who happened to have been born—" he concluded—"into their own class and of their own racial stock."

"Now that we know each other," La Guardia answered back, satisfied, "just forget the whole thing. You are quite right. Some of the highbrows gave me a dirty deal last campaign, yet I am sure you only know half of the story. . . . We will lunch together, and to be sure it is a real roughneck party we will ask Heywood Broun to join us."[8]

In addition to presenting a repellent image to the frock-coat element, La Guardia was handicapped by an unpopular party affiliation in the spring of 1933. Because registered Democrats outnumbered enrolled Republicans by almost four to one, the fusionists intended to run an independent Democrat for mayor. Seabury was the first choice but he declined to be the candidate, giving as his reason that Tammany would accuse him of having launched his investigations for selfish political ambitions. By April the front runner was Joseph V. McKee, president of the Board of Aldermen since 1925 (in 1929 the Citizens Union endorsed his bid for a second term).

One of the few officials of the Walker regime to emerge undirtied from Seabury's muckraking, McKee was a Fordham graduate who had taught at his alma mater and at DeWitt Clinton High School before entering politics in 1918 through the state legislature. As acting mayor for four months between Walker's resignation and O'Brien's inauguration, he brought to City Hall such unusual qualities as energy, seriousness, and intelligence. He made no public protest when the Democratic bosses nominated O'Brien instead of himself to fill Walker's vacancy, but a few weeks after his astonishing write-in vote he delivered a speech so scathingly anti-Tammany that fusionists believed he was ready to break with his party and head their ticket. Like John P. Mitchel, Fusion's last successful mayoralty contender, the Bronx Democrat was young, handsome, well-dressed, educated, Irish, and Catholic.[9]

What was the Italo-American Republican to do? La Guardia had no big press, no big money, no big public relations behind him. The sole organization he commanded was limited to East Harlem and was so heavily Latin as to strengthen the impression that he appealed mostly to his own ethnic group. The truth is that he was known from one end of the city to the other, but the men who counted at the moment knew him as wild and irresponsible and crude. There wasn't the remotest possibility that they would come over to him of their own accord.

They would therefore have to be forced to nominate him, and if that tactic failed, he would have to bypass them through the primary. In either case he would have to show himself as he really was in order to build up public support. He would also have to deal and connive, threaten and strike blows, yet somehow without confirming his stereotype as a roughneck. He would above all else need allies, particularly from the gentry, powerful allies to overcome the fierce resistance of the Fusion Conference Committee's power brokers.

"If it's La Guardia or bust," Joseph Price was to exclaim as late as August 3, "I prefer bust!"[10]

2. Enter Professor Berle

La Guardia's first and most constant ally—the man who believed in him without reservation, introduced him to Seabury, opened still other doors that otherwise would have remained closed to him, bolstered his confidence when things looked blackest, and finally moved his nomination and saw it carried—was a liberal of the New York elite, A. A. Berle, Jr.

A descendant of German Forty-eighters on his father's side and of New Englanders on his mother's, Berle was at thirty-eight a celebrated writer, successful downtown lawyer, professor of corporation law at Columbia University, and Presidential advisor. Since his collaboration with La Guardia in Congress the previous winter, Berle looked up to him as one of the few leaders in American public life who knew *what* had to be done and *how* to get things done. For his own part the politician deferred to the slight, blond, immaculately attired professor. Berle's learning was prodigious, his mind analytical, his eloquence persuasive, and he moved confidently between the worlds of intellect and power.[11]

In late April or May, according to Professor Berle's memory, La Guardia invited him to dinner to talk about his ambitions. There was no need for him to thrash out the pros and cons of the mayoralty and to declare dramatically, "Adolf, I'm going in." Berle, and the public as well, already knew that Fiorello was in the race. But how was he to get the Fusion nomination? The two men agreed that Seabury held the key to the designation, not so much because he sometimes attended the meetings of the Fusion Conference Committee, but because no reform candidate could go before the public without the blessing of Tammany's terrifying biographer.

Berle phoned Seabury a few days later to make an appointment to talk with him at the latter's office at 120 Broadway. Meeting for the first time, the two men nevertheless conversed easily and pleasantly. They came from a similar social background, spoke the same language, had acquaintances and friends in common, and agreed on the need to smash the district leader system in the coming municipal election and redeem the city from Tammany misrule.

"If you want a draft, we're all for it," Berle said after a while. "But if you're out of it and otherwise not committed, I would like to ask for your consideration of a man I have come to respect and admire, Major La Guardia."

Seabury replied that he had renounced all ambitions for the mayoralty when he started his investigations, and that to prevent a draft he recently had changed his residence to East Hampton. He favored no particular candidate at the moment, but was there any truth to the charge, he asked Berle, that La Guardia was a noisy, cheap, self-promoting politician? Recounting his experience in the hectic lame-duck session of the Seventy-second Congress, Berle assured Seabury that the Major had been a model of cool and constructive statesmanship. Seabury promised seriously to consider La Guardia, but did not commit himself to his candidacy.

Shortly thereafter Berle was invited to join a small circle of men around Seabury who ultimately would take the play away from the Fusion Conference Committee. Roy Howard, whose *World-Telegram* had sparked the write-in vote for McKee in 1932, promised his newspaper's support to a suitable Fusion candidate. Three influential Republicans—State Chairman W. Kingsland Macy and former U. S. Attorneys George Z. Medalie and Charles H. Tuttle (the latter had been a 1912 Progressive and G.O.P. gubernatorial contender in 1930)—hoped both to modernize their party and promote Fusion by ousting Old Guard leaders like Whitman. In Professor Berle the Seabury circle added a spokesman, unofficial of course, for innumerable New Deal Democrats.

The grand old man of the group, C. C. (Charles Culp) Burlingham, was also the grand old man of New York City reform. Then eighty-two (he was to reach one hundred

before he died), Burlingham had participated in more causes
for good than his townsmen could remember. Within recent
memory he had been a New Freedom Democrat and peace-
maker in the divisive 1913 Fusion movement. Past president of
the Bar Association, senior warden at St. George's Protestant
Episcopal Church, the friend and patron of Judges Benjamin
Cardozo and Learned Hand, the sort who wrote letters to his
friends in Latin with French quotations, Burlingham embodied
the mugwump tradition at its wisest, mellowest, and most
tolerant. He was known to intimates as C. C. and was one of
the few men who addressed Seabury as Sam.

Berle arranged to have La Guardia meet Seabury, Burlingham, and the others. The Judge was impressed by the Major,
but still he did not commit himself.[12] This was in itself a
victory for La Guardia. He had been given time in which to
maneuver, and in time his more serious rivals eliminated themselves.

McKee was the first to do so. On May 4, 1933, he announced through the press that he was resigning from the
Board of Aldermen and quitting politics for good to take a
bank president's job at a reputed salary of $50,000 a year.
While fusionists were expressing dismay, La Guardia issued a
statement that the "hopes of 6,000,000 people surely cannot be
deflated because one individual has voluntarily removed himself from the fight."

A boom then developed for Al Smith, which La Guardia
publicly supported (he was playing the role of a responsible
man interested only in defeating a crooked machine), but on
condition that Smith put himself at the head of so broad a
coalition as to include such incongruous running mates as
Norman Thomas and John P. O'Brien. On May 15 the Happy
Warrior declared that he was unavailable. La Guardia then
proposed Seabury in a widely reported speech. On the same
day the Judge released a statement to the newspapers that he
would not and could not be drafted.[13]

It was now May 20. La Guardia was still in the running, the
Fusion Conference Committee's hostility to him notwithstanding. Yet he knew that he had survived the first round of
competition only through the default of others. What is more,

a mere three favorites had taken themselves out of the race, and the Conference Committee had barely begun to go down the long list of men deemed eligible. La Guardia had no choice but to go out and fight for the nomination. Mounting a direct assault on the self-designated fusionist leaders, he also and simultaneously put pressure on them through his own Republican Party and the large audience he commanded as an orator.

3. *"Dancing Around and Thundering in the Index"*

From the time he got back to New York City in March until he received the nomination in August, La Guardia spoke up and down the city in order to build up public support and keep his name alive in the newspapers. The master of melting-pot politics addressed a variety of ethnic groups—Negroes and white Anglo-Saxon Protestants, Jews and Italo-Americans, Norwegians, Hungarians, Puerto Ricans, and so on, almost indefinitely. But La Guardia was, and had been, a politician vitally concerned with issues transcending the parochialism of this or that ancestral community. He gave one lecture at Columbia University's School of Journalism on the poor reporting of financial news in the daily press, and another at Yale on the need for massive Government action to roll back the Depression and restore prosperity. The Broadway Temple Methodist church heard him on child welfare; the Salvation Army asked him to appeal for funds over radio station WEAF; *Scribner's* magazine solicited an article from him on the role of the Army and Navy in politics. As the keynote speaker of a meeting chaired by Ambassador James W. Gerard and sponsored by the American National Conference Against Racial Persecution in Germany, La Guardia pronounced Hitler a "perverted maniac."[14]

Meanwhile, he probed for support in the Republican Party. Privately he scorned the local G.O.P., writing to James Marshall that it was "short of ideas and determination,"[15] but he was determined to use it in maneuvering for the nomination. On May 19 he gave a highly publicized talk at the G.O.P. inner sanctum: the 15th Assembly (silk-stocking) District Club. He owed this opportunity to Newbold Morris, the thirty-one-year-old president of the club.

The East Harlem politician met the Central Park East socialite at a dinner party in Adolf Berle's home. The two men were
as different in background and appearance as it is possible to
be. Six feet five, blond and blue-eyed, Morris was a graduate of
the best schools (Groton, Yale College, Columbia University
Law School), a member of an old law firm, and the descendant
of an even older family. One of his ancestors had signed the
Declaration of Independence, his maternal great grandfather
had served as mayor of New York City, and his father had
taken part in Theodore Roosevelt's 1912 Bull Moose movement. Young Morris, too, wanted a career in public service.
Intrigued by the Little Flower, the youthful patrician invited
him to address his club in the hope of launching a La Guardia
boom.[16]

Morris was giving La Guardia a chance to change or at least
soften the image that conservative Republicans had of him as a
dangerous man. Fiorello accepted the challenge, but ap-
proached it fearful of the reception he might have in the
G.O.P. territory most hostile to him in all of New York City.
Many of the silk-hat moneybags who had abandoned him in
1929 lived in the 15th Assembly District, and the ultras among
them raged against Morris for opening the doors of their club
to the "filthy little radical." On May 18 La Guardia wrote to
an old associate in the 15th, Courtlandt Nicoll, imploring him
to attend the meeting:

"I want to have at least one friend in the House, so for
goodness' sake, stand by me just this once."[17]

He arrived ten minutes late to find a large audience waiting
for him. Morris held his breath, afraid that Fiorello might
launch into one of his screaming-soprano, East Harlem ha-
rangues, but the little man began in a voice so low that it could
barely be heard. "I apologize for being late," he said. "Marie,
my wife, sent my suit out to be pressed, and it didn't come
back until a few minutes ago. I couldn't leave the house until it
was returned." The room, glittering with diamonds and evening gowns and boiled shirts, exploded into good-natured
laughter. "I'm very proud to be here tonight," he continued.
"But I don't know whether you ladies and gentlemen have
decided to admit me to the social register," he said slyly but

without sarcasm, "or whether you just wanted to go slumming with me." Again the audience howled, and then sat back to listen.[18]

For in a lightning-fast transition La Guardia moved into a sober discussion of the crisis facing the city. The alternative to oligarchy by crooked Democratic bosses, he started his analysis, was not mismanagement by moribund Republican district leaders. New York required a government by nonpartisan experts, not the exchange of one set of clubhouse loafers for another: an administration based on sound business and executive principles. If he knew that his listeners wanted to hear that message, La Guardia nonetheless and sincerely spoke from the heart. And without directly attacking the Fusion Conference Committee, he called for its enlargement to include women and other unrepresented groups. His candidate for mayor, he concluded quietly, was not himself; it was Judge Seabury.[19]

It is doubtful if La Guardia ever made a more effective speech, and the audience gave him a standing ovation. Asked to prove to an unsympathetic group that he was a sensible political reformer whose character and judgment could be trusted, he succeeded in presenting that side of himself brilliantly. His sense of the meeting had been perfect; or, as one of the club members, Stanley Isaacs, put it: "He had this facility . . . of speaking the way the audience which he was addressing would like him to talk."[20] A T.R. Progressive back in 1912, Isaacs was in August to join Newbold Morris and other Republicans in a maneuver that would enlarge the Fusion Conference Committee and outflank Governor Whitman's unbudgeable opposition to La Guardia.

La Guardia made still another gesture toward Republicans. In the spring of 1933 a band of insurgents led by Chase Mellen, Jr., a thirty-five-year-old socialite and banker, organized themselves into a movement to oust County Chairman Sam Koenig and his district leaders and to pump new life into an ailing organization that had been serving Tammany in exchange for jobs. Fiorello went to see Mellen and his associates and offered to endorse them in the September primary on condition that they endorse him. They refused, explaining that while privately favoring him they could not back him publicly without losing the financial support of Republican fat cats for whom the Little Flower was a dirty word.[21]

Ed Corsi, one of the insurgents, later asked La Guardia, "Why don't you come out for Mellen?"

"Is he ready to come out for me?" Fiorello shot back. "I'm not interested in reforming the Republican party."[22]

Up in East Harlem, at the opposite end of the social scale occupied by the Central Park East 15th Assembly District, there was one Republican organization Fiorello could count on. This was the F. H. La Guardia Political Club, popularly known as the *Gibboni*.* Led by the Major's loyal, shrewd, energetic protégé, Vito Marcantonio, it became the nucleus for a city-wide Latin movement to draft the Little Flower for mayor. Marc circulated petitions for Fiorello in Italo-American neighborhoods from the farthest reaches of Staten Island to the Bronx and sent them, W. Kingsland Macy remembers, "by the wheelbarrow to Seabury." They had an effect. "Macy," Seabury said one day in June, "there seems to be a recurrent demand for La Guardia."[23]

Still other New Yorkers beat the drum for Fiorello on their own initiative. Professor Wallace S. Sayre of New York University, for example, wrote to Seabury that La Guardia was not only the most able campaigner available to Fusion, but that he also had a splendid record, was a sincere and well-informed progressive, would appeal to the left, and could command the allegiance of some 400,000 voters in the Italian colony. "This group, I am convinced from studies of electoral behavior in New York City, is the most important to Fusion—" Sayre emphasized—"for it is both highly cohesive and in a mood for revolt against the dominant machine."[24]

---

* Tammany regarded the name as sinister and accused La Guardia of retaining an assortment of Mafia cutthroats and gorillas. But the truth is that there were no gangsters, and the term Gibboni had the most innocent derivation. After winning a baseball game the Club earned the reputation of being "*campioni*" (champions), Judge Eugene Canudo has written, but "one of the Club's kibitzers remarked on one occasion that to him they looked more like 'gibboni' (referring to the Gibbon ape) than campioni. Everyone laughed at this and the term somehow stuck. Before long most of the members were referring to one another as 'gibboni' and the name became standard East Harlemese for 'member of the F. H. La Guardia Political Club.' " Canudo to Author, August 26, 1957.

Meanwhile the Fusion Conference Committee was ignoring
La Guardia, or, more accurately, trying to. Recovering from
the shock of McKee's withdrawal, Whitman, Price, Davidson,
and Smull (sometimes joined by others of their respective
groups) met weekly at the Luncheon Club, 40 Wall Street, to
assess the field of independent Democrats and, what is more to
the point, to persuade one of them to run. By the third week
of July they had sounded out a highly respected social worker
(Raymond V. Ingersoll); an NBC vice-president (Richard C.
Patterson, Jr.); a public-spirited realtor (Peter Grimm); a
Federal judge (John C. Knox); a bank president (George V.
McLaughlin); a former State Supreme Court Justice (Clarence
J. Shearn); the scion of a celebrated merchant family (Nathan
Straus, Jr.)—all told, more than a dozen men.

One and all declined, giving a variety of explanations for
being unavailable. Ingersoll's reason was health. Patterson said
that his firm disapproved of his mixing politics with business.
Straus was afraid that, with Herbert Lehman governor of the
state, anti-Semites would be aroused if still another Jew were
to run for high office in New York. But whatever the individual reasons, none of the candidates wanted to be mayor
fiercely enough to give up his party loyalty or sacrifice his
personal, professional, or business life to the brutality and
uncertainties of a campaign and the backbreaking office that
was its prize.[25]

"We went all the way down the line," Davidson has remarked in his reminiscences, "and we couldn't get anybody.
All the time this was happening, Fiorello H. La Guardia was
standing in the wings—not standing, but moving around very,
very rapidly. He would send for me every once in a while and
say, 'How are you getting on?' I had not known him. It
doesn't take long to get to know him. . . . He would say,
'Well, who's your latest mayor?' and I would tell him. He
would jump around and shake his fist and he'd say, 'Well,
there's only one man going to be the candidate, and I'm the
man. I'm going to run. I want to be mayor.'"

La Guardia threatened that, if the Fusion Conference Committee bypassed him for someone he judged unsuitable, he
would split the reform movement by entering the election as

an independent. Other than Seabury, who was of course out of the running, La Guardia thought no one suitable, or else he laid down conditions, as he did with Al Smith, no candidate could accept.

Here is how Davidson later put it: "La Guardia . . . was dancing around and thundering in the index about what he was going to do. He wanted the nomination! He wanted it! God! Nobody else wanted it! They were afraid of it—afraid of being licked, afraid they couldn't carry it through. There were lots of reasons they always gave, sometimes personal. But here we had a man all the time who knew he wanted it. He wanted it!"[26]

But no matter how much he wanted *it*, no matter how often he bullied the Fusion Conference Committee for *it*, no matter how strenuously he went after *it* by lining up Italo-American support, courting silk-stocking Republicans, and appealing to the public, Fiorello would be unable to get that nomination unless and until he enjoyed the patronage of the one man in New York City who alone possessed the leverage to boost him over the top.

4. *Breakthrough*

"Sam," Seabury's sister-in-law asked him, "how did you possibly come to pick La Guardia to run for mayor?"

"Because," Seabury answered, "he's absolutely honest, he's a man of great courage, and he can win."[27]

No more than in many other turning points in history resting on human decisions can one say precisely when Seabury made up his mind to throw his immense weight behind La Guardia. Whenever the subject came up in later years, Seabury insisted that he had favored Fiorello all along. That was also how La Guardia remembered the order of events. "All I know was that Judge Seabury was the only one who was for me in the beginning, in the middle and up to the very end," he wrote in 1943 to C. C. Burlingham, who was preparing a pamphlet about the 1933 Fusion nomination.

Yet La Guardia's word cannot be accepted as clinching the point. "Really," he told Burlingham, "I do not know much

about the inside working and the personalities you mention.
. . . I really haven't any information that would be helpful.
My part really started after the designation."[28]

Professor Berle, whose role began earlier as the initial link
between the Major and the Judge, stated in an interview in
1960 that Seabury thought long as well as hard before deciding
to come out for La Guardia. The evidence supports Berle. If
Seabury had always been for La Guardia, it is hard to explain
why he didn't block the Fusion Conference Committee's tend-
ering the nomination to a dozen and more other men. As late
as July 22, 1933, when it was offered to Nathan Straus, Jr.,
Seabury not only didn't object, but according to Morris Ernst
actually advised Straus to accept the designation.[29]

At about the same time in July Rufus E. McGahen, who
sometimes sat in on the Fusion Conference Committee as
secretary of the Citizens Union and as an officer of the City
Fusion Party, went out to East Hampton to have a talk with
Seabury. In 1959 he described their conversation in this way:
"I particularly favored General O'Ryan and also Bob Moses
(in the light of his amazing administrative accomplishment at
Albany). I found Judge Seabury unfriendly to both suggestions and he seemed to agree with me that La Guardia was
clearly not qualified for the mayoralty. He kept repeating,
however, that the first necessity was to pick someone who
could make a winning fight for election."

If McGahen's memory played tricks on him, it was not due
to malice. He served in the La Guardia administration for the
full twelve years, as budget director, deputy mayor, and in
other capacities, and came to regard La Guardia "with the
deepest admiration, respect and complete devotion." When in
1959 he composed the lines quoted above, he looked back upon
his years with Fiorello as the most exciting and rewarding in
his life.[30]

Sources *contemporary* to the event corroborate McGahen's
and Berle's recollections that Seabury was not for La Guardia
in the beginning and in the middle. On July 15 C. C. Burlingham informed his old friend Richard Welling, the founder of
the Good Government clubs in the 1890's and a member of the

advisory council of the City Fusion Party, that Seabury "wonders whether businessmen would accept La Guardia. He is not *heartily* for La Guardia." On July 22 Welling wrote to Ben Howe, director of organization of the City Fusion Party, that the "oldest and wisest sage in town [presumably Burlingham] tells me that S. S. does not want La Guardia, but wants someone to head Fusion who is going after it hotfoot and not someone who needs to be asked." Why not, therefore, draft Seabury? Howe's answer two days later was:

> I have yours of the 22nd and am sorry to say in reply that you are laboring under the same misapprehension that seems to have taken hold of the City, namely, that Judge Seabury has not been sufficiently urged to run for Mayor. He was told that a meeting was under way to fill the Yankee Stadium in one grand acclaim drafting him for Mayor and he positively put his foot down on it and stopped it. Now, if you can think of anything of a more dynamic urge, please name it. Not only is his answer "No," but he is now disqualified. He must live in the county four months and that qualifying date has passed. As much as I hate to admit it, the whole matter is settled. He is leaving for Europe as soon as the candidate is named and I fear we cannot count very much on him to help us in the campaign.
>
> Needless to say, we are very much confused about a suitable candidate. Everybody seems to know the available candidate that we should not name, but no one comes forth with an available candidate who we can agree upon and who will run. Straus would have been admirable, but has definitely declined. All leading Jews agree that they will not stand for a Jew candidate owing to the Nazi furor it might raise. They claim that a Jewish governor and a Jewish mayor would cause a kickback.
>
> . . . Frankly, while I know all the answers against La Guardia's candidacy, he seems to be the only available candidate.
>
> I am afraid your "sage" is not very well informed. It is true that Seabury is not hotfoot for La Guardia, but, it seems to be going to La Guardia by default. I would like to ask you what you think would happen if we turned La Guardia down on the ground that we do not want an Italian

for Mayor at this particular time when the Italians have such a big chest. You can imagine what Generoso Pope would do with his three Italian newspapers screaming about La Guardia being turned down because he was an italian [*sic*]. We are in a tough spot I can assure you.[31]

Not until the wild week leading up to the climactic night of August 3–4, when the contest narrowed down to La Guardia, Robert Moses, founder of the New York State park system, and General John F. O'Ryan, World War I commander of the Twenty-seventh Division, did Seabury come out fighting for Fiorello.

On July 26, without informing Seabury beforehand, the Fusion Conference Committee agreed to designate Moses. Seabury was not only stunned, he was furious. He had been sounded out earlier in the month about Moses and had expressed such vehement opposition that Joseph Price, Moses's principal sponsor, wrote to Richard Welling on July 18 that the park commissioner's candidacy seemed doomed. Seabury disapproved of Moses because the latter was contemptuous of proportional representation, indeed of Goo Goo reforms in general, and also because he was a protégé of Al Smith, a sachem of the hated Hall.[32]

Seabury met Davidson, head of the City Fusion Party, for lunch at the Bankers Club on July 27 to demand the nomination for La Guardia. It was impossible, Davidson said, for Whitman would never agree to the Little Flower. "You sold out to Tammany Hall," Seabury shouted, pounding the table and rattling the dishes. "I'll denounce you and everybody else. You sold out the movement to Tammany Hall." He stood up and walked out without finishing his meal. Davidson followed him, remonstrating, but Seabury would hear no more. "You sold out. Good-bye," he said as the elevator door closed.[33]

La Guardia, by now meeting daily with Seabury, was amazed that the Conference Committee had dared to defy his patron by picking Moses. "I will stand shoulder to shoulder with Judge Samuel Seabury," he told the press, but added in a statesmanlike manner that he was still prepared to back a genuine anti-Tammany candidate other than himself.[34]

Meanwhile, Moses was having a talk with the man he regarded as *his* patron, Al Smith. Although an independent Republican, Moses had been one of the governor's right-hand men in Albany, and believed that Smith owed it to him to support him in the campaign. But that's not the way the Happy Warrior played the game. A regular, he said that it was out of the question for him to back a candidate other than his own Democratic Party's (actually he was to endorse no one in 1933). Moses telephoned Joseph Price to withdraw his name.[35]

The Fusion Conference Committee then turned to O'Ryan. Attending a conference in Chicago when notified he had been chosen, O'Ryan accepted and left immediately for New York City. Once again Seabury, as Burlingham put it, "blew his trumpet blast."[36] The general, then a lawyer and vice-chairman of the City Fusion Party, wouldn't do: he was politically inexperienced, colorless, conservative, an advocate of a higher subway fare—hardly the sort, protested Seabury, to wage a fighting campaign and win a popular mandate.

These were valid objections, but something else was involved: the bad blood between Seabury and Whitman dating back to the 1916 governor's race. "I had no knowledge at all a day or two ago," O'Ryan wrote to Welling on August 3, "of the existing feud between the Governor and the Judge. . . ."[37] The fusionist movement had reached an impasse; neither Whitman nor Seabury was capable of agreeing on a candidate whom the other preferred. Whitman was not only O'Ryan's most emphatic booster, he was also La Guardia's most vehement detractor. As for Seabury, he denounced his enemy's favoring O'Ryan as "a complete and disgraceful sell-out to Tammany Hall."

La Guardia, still pretending that his only concern was that Fusion pick a candidate who could beat Tammany, declared for the press that the "momentary issue is between the judgement, sincerity, vision, unselfishness of Mr. Charles Whitman and Judge Samuel Seabury."[38]

That was not the issue of the moment, as Fiorello well knew. The immediate question was which of the two power brokers, the Judge or the Governor, was going to smash the resistance of the other. On August 2 the Seabury circle made two maneuvers, one designed to eliminate Whitman and O'Ryan from the battleground, and the other to weaken the Fusion Conference Committee.

Kingsland Macy broke off a salmon fishing vacation in Canada to hurry back to New York City. He implored O'Ryan to withdraw his name, explaining that Seabury's opposition would wreck not only his own candidacy but also the cause of Fusion. O'Ryan promised to do so only if the Republican Mayoralty Committee, headed by Governor Whitman and planning to meet on the following day, failed to give him a "convincing unanimity." Macy made plans with Charles Tuttle and others of the Committee not to give the general that kind of unanimity.

Also on August 2, a "harmony committee" was formed on the initiative of Roy Howard, George Medalie, C. C. Burlingham, and Seabury to supersede but also to include the Fusion Conference Committee. Burlingham was the chairman. Three members of the new group were openly for La Guardia: Seabury, Berle, Newbold Morris (and probably Burlingham by this time). Three others could be expected to stand by O'Ryan: Price, Davidson, Smull (Whitman was invited but refused to join). As for the others, James E. Finegan of the City Fusion Party; J. G. L. Molloy of the Knickerbocker (anti-Tammany) Democrats; Robert McC. Marsh, representing the anti-Koenig Republicans; and William Schieffelin, chairman of the Citizens Union—only time would tell how they would vote.[39]

La Guardia issued a press release saying that, if refused the designation, he would fight it out with O'Ryan in the Republican primary, and if defeated, in the election as an independent. But there was no fuse to the bomb. The scrappy little man believed the game was up and that a dark horse would emerge as a compromise Fusion choice.

That's how he expressed himself over dinner at Professor Berle's town house on East Nineteenth Street near Gramercy Park. Looking like a man for whom the gates of heaven had been opened and then slammed in his face, he said: "You'll propose me, they'll propose O'Ryan, and then we'll both have

to withdraw for some nonentity who will get the nomination."
Berle tried in vain to reassure him that Seabury and Burlingham were fighters and would put him over; Fiorello insisted
that his political career was over. He was through. Of that he
was certain.

After dinner the two men walked uptown in the warm
summer night. "Why is it that every time you get to a point
where you can do some good the *nice people* move in and
block you?" La Guardia asked bitterly. "That's what drives a
man like me to be a demagogue, smacking into things."[40]

The deadlock was broken between the afternoon of August
3 and the early hours of August 4.

The Republican Mayoralty Committee met on August 3 at
the National Republican Club, with Governor Whitman presiding. He introduced a resolution endorsing General O'Ryan,
but Ed Corsi and Vito Marcantonio lined up with Charles
Tuttle and Stanley Isaacs to filibuster against the motion. "The
one man Tammany is afraid of is Seabury," argued Tuttle.
"The man whose support can elect our ticket is Seabury. Why
take action here which Tammany would give its eye-teeth to
have us take? Rightly or wrongly, Mr. Seabury has taken his
position. We are now proposing to open our campaign by
taking a slap at Judge Seabury."

The long and stormy afternoon ended without anyone
receiving a Republican endorsement. Instead an uncommitted
delegation, led by Kingsland Macy and Tuttle (both of the
Seabury circle), was authorized to join the Burlingham (harmony) Committee meeting at 6 P.M. that evening at the Bar
Association Building.[41]

That session, too, was heated. Offered the nomination once
again, Seabury again refused it. The majority was for O'Ryan,
but Seabury wouldn't have him. Other candidates were considered, but Seabury found reasons to object to them, too. "Sit
down, Sam, sit down," Burlingham implored his friend during
one angry exchange—to the astonishment of Davidson and the
others at hearing Seabury called by his first name. Finally,
after some six hours of wrangling, Berle moved the designation
of La Guardia and talked eloquently about the former Con-

gressman's magnificent work in Washington the previous winter to halt foreclosures and bankruptcy. Seabury seconded the nomination.

At a few minutes past midnight, with Price, Davidson, and Smull still holding out, the majority agreed on La Guardia.

After telephoning O'Ryan, who magnanimously released his supporters in order to promote unity, Davidson changed his vote. The Republican and City Fusion Parties made it official the next day, giving Fiorello two lines on the ballot. Price was eventually to come around, too, despite his angry protest to the press on leaving the meeting that "the conference was absolutely dominated by the attitude of Judge Seabury, who would accept no other name besides Congressman La Guardia's. . . ."[42]

Fiorello was at home with Marcantonio, Ed Corsi, and other friends while his political future dangled in the balance before the Burlingham Committee. The evening was long, tense, and silent. Shortly after midnight the telephone rang. Seabury was at the other end of the line. Joy, mingled with relief but also with surprise and even disbelief, swept the room. La Guardia and his Italo-American associates had doubted, down to the last minute, that the Nice People could be forced to give up their stereotype of the Little Flower as a Little Wop.

"I promise you faithfully you will never regret this," La Guardia said to Seabury. "I hope I shall be able to make you proud of me."[43]

5. *Men, Not Institutions*

Even now it is hard to disentangle the variables in the equation of La Guardia's nomination and assign an order of priority to them. Influence, prejudice, grudge, ambition—as well as a sincere desire to cleanse New York City—were all involved. The best of human nature mingled with the worst in putting Fiorello over. And in so human an enterprise it is not surprising that he should also have benefited from timing, accident, chance—in plainer language from just plain luck. La Guardia was lucky that Seabury, and all the other candidates favored above him, had shown no stomach for the office he had been dreaming of occupying ever since breaking into politics as an election district captain before World War I.

Institutions were unimportant in themselves in deciding the outcome. When Fiorello threw his hat into the arena in March, the institutions he desperately needed—the Fusion Conference Committee, the Republican Party, the City Fusion Party, the Good Government associations, the business community—closed their doors in his face. La Guardia himself helped to open them; Berle and Morris and then others pried them further apart; Seabury finally smashed them down. Using institutions for their own ends, La Guardia and his allies were men with a taste for combat, a talent for maneuver, a habit of commanding, and a sense of direction.

La Guardia was the beneficiary of that direction. The occasion called for a rough-and-tumble campaigner, and the brawler from East Harlem had demonstrated that he could beat the Tiger at its own game. The times demanded a progressive leader, and Fiorello had been known for years as "America's Most Liberal Congressman." He was an appropriate rallying point for the coalition that finally jelled around him: New Dealers (Berle, Roy Howard, Molloy and Finegan); Progressive Era veterans (the New Freedom Democrats Burlingham and Seabury and the New Nationalist Republicans Isaacs and Tuttle); modern Republicans (Macy and Morris); and the Good Government associations (Davidson and Schieffelin).

If La Guardia was the reluctant, distasteful, last-minute choice forced on the gentry, he was nevertheless their choice. In the months ahead he would face the problem in reverse. Would the man in the street overcome his prejudice against Goo Goos? They had a reputation for being impractical, ineffective, snobbish, and were known as losers. La Guardia entered the campaign knowing that he would have to expand his coalition if he was to offer himself as the candidate of *all* the people.

IV

The Campaign of 1933

There were to be moments of anxiety during the campaign and even of heartbreak and panic for the excitable little man with the expressive face and earnest mission, but in the opening round extending from the August 4 designation to the September 19 primaries, his mood was confident as the signs mounted that he had not only a winning issue but the wherewithal to carry his cause into every part of the city and an easy opponent to beat.

1. *Everything Going for Him*

Fusion headquarters were established in the Paramount Building on Times Square, and in a matter of weeks La Guardia built a city-wide organization. The press generously publicized his activities, but Tammany was so sure of itself that it ignored him. Even while he was mounting a voter registration drive that would jump enrollment to a record high, the Hall operated on the principle that there would be the usual light vote in a municipal election and that the majority of New Yorkers who bothered to go to the polls would as in the past do so as gut Democrats. In contrast to the cosmopolitan and able ticket put together by Fiorello and his Fusion associates, the Democratic bosses fielded a slate not only predominantly Celtic but sprinkled with veterans of the

Tin Box Brigade. The most accurate index to the cynical overconfidence of Tammany Hall was its choice of a mayoral candidate. Whereas Seabury had forced La Guardia on reform as the man most likely to win, John F. Curry had John P. O'Brien renamed over Ed Flynn's warning that he was sure to lose.[1]

On September 1 a New York *Daily News* straw poll revealed that the Fusion challenger was off to a running headstart over the Tammany incumbent.

John Patrick O'Brien had been exposed to the public for almost a year, and in the summer of 1933 Alva Johnston expressed the consensus of journalists that he belonged "to the Organization's upper ten per cent in character and to its upper fifty per cent in ability." No one within recent memory had worked harder or more sincerely at being mayor, but although not stupid, the sixty-year-old politician had not been intelligent enough to cope with the problems inherited from the Walker administrations and accentuated by the Depression. Within months of taking office he was forced to mortgage the city's finances to the bankers. What is more, in spite of his degrees from Holy Cross and Georgetown and his pride at being a scholar in politics, O'Brien displayed a mastery of the misplaced phrase, and the press did him the disservice of quoting him accurately.

The result was that he confronted La Guardia not only as a failure in office but also as the author of malapropisms that had won him the unenviable title of the year's clown of the town. It was on record that the mayor had hailed Einstein as "that scientist of scientists, Albert Weinstein"; that he had tried to cultivate a Negro audience by describing Harlem as "the garden spot of New York"; that he had baffled a Greek-American gathering with the boast that he had won a medal in college for translating "that great Greek poet, Horace." Other politicians have made slips of the tongue, and surely to the extent of mistaking Roman for Greek writers, but reporters have straightened out their mistakes. In O'Brien's case the press concluded very early in his administration that he was a comic in spite of himself and, therefore, fair game for entertaining copy. The news cameras also caricatured him. Failing to capture the mayor's alert blue eyes or affable expression, they distorted his large jaw, protruding brow, prominent bald head, and barrel-chested build, so that he often looked like first cousin to Piltdown man. That's how he sounded to the cynical members of the fourth estate assigned to City Hall when he confessed: "Oh, I would love to be a newspaperman, because I love the classics and I love good literature."

His ingenuousness rendered him incapable of perceiving the unintentioned humor of his utterances. After Seabury had sent Walker packing, O'Brien advised New York City's youth to "join Tammany Hall and work for it." The reason? "Reward will come." When a Madison Square Garden convention of Democratic committeemen chose him (the word had been sent down by Boss Curry) to replace Walker, the poor boy from Worcester, Massachusetts, who had made good philosophized: "It was like a New England town meeting. It was marvelous to see the unanimity of those thirty thousand people." Although entering City Hall with a proclamation of political independence, he blurted out when asked by a reporter who his police commissioner would be: "I don't know. I haven't got the word yet."[2]

The strategy La Guardia adopted was to treat O'Brien as Curry's puppet and to hammer away at both the incompetence and the corruption of the Hall. It was to be a contest against "the Blunderbird and the Plunderbird." In August Fiorello made a tactical decision to saturate the electorate in a short but intensive campaign to open formally on October 2 at historic Cooper Union. It was there, sixty years before, that the movement had been launched to smash the Tweed Ring.

Friends, well-wishers, and associates advised Fiorello to base the campaign on other issues besides Tammany misrule, but throughout August and September he dismissed all such counsel as unrelated to the business of throwing the rascals out of office. When asked by the Association of Foreign Language Newspaper Editors for his social and economic views, he replied that they were irrelevant: "The only question is honest and efficient administration of our municipal government." When urged to go after the conservative vote, he responded that it had no choice but to seek him: "God help conservatives if Tammany Hall continues for four more years in office. They have everything at stake. I only have four terrible, hard, trying, heart-breaking years ahead of me." When counseled to capitalize on his father's Army service, he snapped that he would do nothing of the sort: "If you want my father's military record, you can have it—but he is dead—he is not running for office. I am."

"There is only one issue," La Guardia emphasized the point for fellow Fusion candidates at a Hotel Astor luncheon on September 14, "and that issue is the Tammany Hall of John F. Curry."[3]

But he did agree, because it corresponded to his own way of thinking, with the suggestion to select running mates from every numerically important ethnic group in town. Except for minor concessions to the Jewish vote, Tammany had long been making nominations and appointments on the boast that "the Irish are natural leaders" and that other groups "want to be ruled by them." No less anachronistic was Curry's belief that Manhattan held the other boroughs as satellites. The census returns revealed, as La Guardia well knew, that Manhattan had lost population since 1920 to Brooklyn, Queens, and the Bronx; and that the Irish were outnumbered by the Italians, who in turn were exceeded by the Jews. And he knew also that a sizable minority of old-stock Americans of Protestant persuasion (for the most part Republican) resented their lack of representation in the municipal government since the Mitchel administration of twenty years before.

For the first time an Italian, an Irishman, a Jew, and a white Anglo-Saxon Protestant ran on the same ticket for the four top positions. Never before had so carefully and ethnically contrived a ticket been offered to the New York City electorate. It was balanced in other ways as well. Fiorello's choice for comptroller, Major W. Arthur Cunningham, was an independent Democrat and Queens banker whom the *Fusion Handbook* publicized as a World War I hero and as an officer of the Father Duffy Chapter of the famed Rainbow Division's veterans association. Bernard S. Deutsch, the candidate for president of the Board of Alderman, was a lawyer who doubled as chairman of the Bronx's City Fusion Party and president of the American Jewish Congress. For District Attorney of New York County Fusion nominated a Manhattan Republican of colonial Dutch origins, Jacob Gould Schurman, Jr., whose father had been president of Cornell University and Ambassador to China and Germany.

La Guardia's running mates for the five borough presidencies were also chosen with an eye for ethnic, religious, and political considerations. The Ulster-born incumbent of Queens, George U. Harvey, brought a personal Republican machine to the cause of Fusion. The other four men were independent Democrats. Joseph A. Palma of Staten Island, a successful businessman and former Secret Service agent, was an Italo-American Catholic in a borough more heavily Latin than most. Two old-stock Americans, Langdon W. Post and Raymond V. Ingersoll, the one the head of the Knickerbocker Democrats and the other a founder of the City Fusion Party, were the respective candidates in Manhattan and Brooklyn. The Bronx designee, Charles P. Barry, was a balanced ticket in himself. Born in Vermont of Irish parents, he taught government at N.Y.U. where, according to the *Fusion Handbook*, he was the treasurer not only of his own Newman Society but of the Jewish Menorah Society, the Protestant Christian Association, and the Inter-Faith Council as well.[4]

The fusionists prided themselves on playing smart politics, but what did their ticket have to do with good government? It is not enough to say that, in a pluralist society where bloc voting is a hard fact of political life, La Guardia pandered to parochialism as a necessary step toward winning public office. More to the point was his success, *on the whole*, in choosing men of genuine ability. Fiorello played the averages. Apart from Palma and Harvey, the one picked mainly for ethnic reasons and the other primarily for party affiliation, La Guardia and his running mates would have graced any local reform slate in the country then or now.

Raymond Ingersoll had been prodding the civic conscience for more than thirty years—as a settlement house resident in the 1890's and as a magistrate elected with Seth Low in 1901, as a park commissioner in the Mitchel administration, an advisor to Al Smith, and as an arbitrator in New York City's garment industry from 1925 to 1931. If Barry was politically untried except for being a college administrator and an officer of the City Fusion Party, it was all the more refreshing for an attractive young political science professor to challenge a Tammany hack. At only thirty-four Langdon Post had distinguished himself in the state assembly and as a New Deal relief official. Deutsch was an outstanding member of the bar, Schurman had been Seabury's right-hand man in the investigations, and Cunningham would bring years of banking experience to the comptrollership.

Cunningham knew little about municipal finance, however, and the expert on that subject, Professor Joseph D. McGoldrick of Columbia University, who wanted the nomination for comptroller and would get it the next time round, has told the story that in 1933 he lost out to the tall and handsome war hero because he was built altogether too much like the Little Flower. "After all," La Guardia later quipped to him, "we couldn't run two short stouts on the same ticket!"[5]

Fiorello was euphoric after the September 19 primaries, for not only did he and his fellows win that first test at the polls, but bossism suffered so severe a beating that La Guardia hailed it as an omen for the November outcome. An uprising in the Republican primary overthrew the ancient and mouldy Koenig machine, and Chase Mellen, the thirty-five-year-old insurgent who replaced Koenig as Manhattan's G.O.P. leader, pledged the support of a reformed organization to Fusion. As for the Democrats, O'Brien squeaked by against unprecedented but divided opposition, three of eight Tammany incumbent district leaders were sent into retirement, and the organization's designee for comptroller fell before a Brooklyn apostate standing for office independently of the party's standard bearer. In contrast, the Fusion ticket entered the lists unchallenged and emerged intact and unified.[6]

By the last week in September La Guardia's lead over O'Brien in the *Literary Digest* poll had soared to four to one,[7] and Tammany district leaders were muttering that their man couldn't go the distance. The press, outside New York as well as inside the city, acclaimed Fusion and predicted a November sweep for Fusion. But La Guardia's hopes for a joyous romp

over a bumbling opponent suddenly disintegrated when the
character of the campaign radically changed as a result of a
power play by the master politician who had been following
the New York scene from the White House.

2. *Temporary Panic*

The results of the September primaries were no sooner
known than President Franklin D. Roosevelt sent for Jim
Farley and Ed Flynn and told them to persuade Joe McKee to
return to public life and run for mayor. Postmaster General
Farley's several political duties included being chairman of the
New York State Democratic Party, and Flynn's Bronx was the
sole New York City county organization loyal to the President.
The White House conclave was supposed to be secret but it
made the newspapers on September 23, and for the remainder
of the week La Guardia and his associates frantically appealed
to McKee and his boosters not to put another anti-Curry ticket
in the field. They appealed in vain. Farley denied being party to
a McKee boom, and Roosevelt refused to see Fiorello's emissaries, proclaiming through press secretary Steve Early a policy of strict neutrality in the local campaign!

McKee entered the race on September 30. The candidate of
the newly created Recovery Party, he declared that "the
people of New York City want in the municipal government
what they now have in the nation—a new deal." Two days
later the press reported that his campaign manager would be
Harry M. Durning: collector of the New York City Port,
distributor of Federal patronage, and a Roosevelt appointee.[8]

Why did F.D.R. intervene?

It has been said, most recently by one of his biographers,
that he intervened with the purpose of assuring La Guardia's
victory by splitting the Democratic vote.[9] That may have
been his Machiavellian stratagem, but there is no documentary
proof that it was. It is more likely, as Flynn and Farley have
written, that the President wanted to win with McKee in
order to prevent a Republican victory and also to take away
the New York City Democratic Party from a machine not
merely corrupt and embarrassing but disloyal and inept as

well. In 1932 Curry and the other county leaders, excepting
Ed Flynn, had opposed Roosevelt's nomination for President
and Herbert Lehman's for governor; and now the same rascally and foolish crowd was running a loser for mayor who by
November promised to turn over the biggest Democratic city
in America to a nominal Republican officially endorsed by the
G.O.P.[10] With the state's organization already subject to the
White House through Farley and Lehman, the President
would control the city's through Flynn and McKee.

But whatever Roosevelt's motives, his action shattered La
Guardia's euphoria. The man to beat was no longer the foot-in-
the-mouth O'Brien, discredited and defenseless and all but
repudiated by his own party primary; it was McKee, the man
who had rung up nearly a quarter of a million write-in votes in
1932. There was a danger that the erstwhile banker would
appeal to conservative Republican businessmen who had
grudgingly accepted La Guardia because Seabury had given
them no other choice. More seriously, McKee threatened to
divide with La Guardia both the independent vote and the anti-
Curry Democratic vote.[11] New Yorkers could remember that,
only a few months before, Fusion had ranked the young Bronx
Democrat as a mayoralty hope second only to the mighty
Seabury. And no matter what Steve Early said to the contrary,
McKee seemed to enjoy the confidence of a President who had
just swept New York City with an awesome 67 per cent
majority.

Once again as on the eve of the Burlingham Committee
meeting in August to decide the nomination, Fiorello slid into
a fit of depression. But the despair passed as he threw himself
into the task of shaping a suitable strategy against McKee. The
essence of that strategy was to attack his opponent again and
again as the Bronx mouthpiece for Tammany Hall. Two weeks
after McKee's entry La Guardia's instinct for the jugular was
so active that, as we shall later see in detail, he hurled a charge
of anti-Semitism against his Recovery opponent so serious as
to send McKee reeling and drive a wedge between him and the
White House.

But even before then, with regard to such campaign essen-
tials as running mates, advisors, organization, voter registration, and poll watchers, La Guardia held all of the advantages.

McKee's was supposed to be a nonpartisan and balanced ticket,* but unlike La Guardia's, it contained no Republicans, no City Fusion Partyites, no members of Seabury's staff, and no Anglo-Saxon Protestants. It was not only a Democratic slate, the Recovery label notwithstanding; it was also incomplete. Entering the contest as late as he did McKee was unable to mount a full contingent of aldermanic nominees or even to fill all the candidacies for the borough presidencies. Therefore, if elected he would not have, as La Guardia would if he carried his team into office, a majority on the Board of Aldermen or a full Board of Estimate. The latter, consisting of the mayor, the comptroller, the president of the Board of Aldermen, and the five borough presidents, was the city's chief legislative as well as executive body.

Nor was McKee able to match La Guardia's organization on the staff level. In addition to Seabury, Burlingham, Berle, and Roy Howard, who continued a harmonious collaboration begun in the spring, La Guardia's board of strategists included Paul Windels, his manager in the 1919 campaign for aldermanic president, and William M. Chadbourne, a veteran of the 1912 Bull Moose and 1913 Fusion movements. This small, congenial, and able group met the candidate daily for breakfast at either Seabury's or Chadbourne's home to talk over policy. It was at one such session that the decision was made to meet the Recovery threat by labeling McKee as boss Flynn's puppet.[12]

Not that McKee's advisors were inferior to La Guardia's as individuals. Professor Raymond Moley had just finished a tour of duty on the New Deal brain trust; Herbert Bayard Swope possessed a knowledge of local affairs gained from having published the old New York *World;* George V. McLaughlin was a former member of Al Smith's administration; W. Averell Harriman would shortly be President Roosevelt's Ambassador to Russia; Jim Farley and Ed Flynn excelled of course as professional politicians; and so it went for a half dozen or so other men.

* The Recovery candidate for district attorney was Ferdinand Pecora, who was well known in the Italian colony, and the designee for president of the Board of Aldermen was Nathan Straus, Jr., the man who had turned down the Fusion nomination for mayor out of fear that a Jewish mayor would incite anti-Semitism (see pp. 79, 82).

But unlike La Guardia's inner circle, the men around McKee engaged each other in tedious and acrimonious debates unproductive of positive policy. "Each man was an individualist," Flynn later complained, "and had his own ideas of how to run a campaign." More than that, in the haste to overcome Fusion's two-month headstart, the men who masterminded the Recovery campaign managed to make—McLaughlin told Seabury after the election—"all the mistakes in the political calendar and some that had never previously been thought of." Perhaps things would have turned out otherwise had Ed Flynn been able openly to take charge, but "boss" was such a dirty word in the fall of 1933 that the Bronx leader was afraid to show himself at McKee's headquarters. Instead he met clandestinely with Recovery's strategists in the evening at the Hotel Roosevelt. There, amidst violent discussions, he tried in vain, as he later wrote, "to get some semblance of unity and organization into the campaign."[13]

With Flynn's failure to line up McCooey's Brooklyn machine behind Recovery, La Guardia was assured of having much the larger field organization. McKee's major organizational strength lay in Flynn's Bronx, and O'Brien's in Curry's Manhattan. In the other three boroughs, although the county chairmen remained nominally loyal to O'Brien, enough assembly district leaders and election district captains broke for McKee to shatter party unity.[14] The exact proportions are unknown, but neither McKee nor O'Brien could count on more than a fraction of the once formidable Democratic army of thirty-two thousand committeemen.

La Guardia had at least twice that number of men and women working for him. Some did so through their own City Fusion or Republican Parties on the county, assembly district, or election district levels. Others got out the vote through the already established Knickerbocker Democrats or such *ad hoc* groups as the Roosevelt Democrats for La Guardia or New Deal Democrats for La Guardia. Still others made a contribution through the multitudinous committees set up by Fiorello's managers for women, ethnic groups, fraternal societies, the professions, businessmen, workers, and so on across the economic and sociological spectrum. No class, no occupation, no social stratum of any kind was overlooked. When the National

Association of the Deaf gathered for a political symposium, La Guardia sent over Fusion speakers (!) and organizers to attend.

It fell to Vito Marcantonio, Ed Corsi, and Leonard Covello to swing the Italian colony behind Fiorello. But there was no need to organize the Italo-Americans. Going wild over their hero's candidacy, they organized themselves, tens and hundreds and even thousands of them converting their lodges, churches, trade unions, businesses, neighborhoods, athletic teams, and extended families into campaign machinery for La Guardia. He encouraged one and all, caring not whether they were Socialists, Anarchists, Fascists, or Political Apathetics. Over in Queens insurance salesmen advertised his cause while selling policies to Latin family heads. Along the Brooklyn waterfront, in the Little Italy of the Ninth Assembly District, an F. H. La Guardia Political Club suddenly sprang into existence with a membership just short of a thousand. From Greenwich Village, where the Little Flower had lived until 1921, a campaign worker wrote:

"You never thought, of course, when you used to give those boxes of spaghetti to my poor children at 49 Charles Street that it would be a trump card for you. I am playing it for all I am worth—talk about 'casting bread upon the waters'—what about spaghetti?"[15]

There was muscle as well as *pasta* in the La Guardia organization. The Honest Ballot Association marched out some twenty-thousand strong during registration week and again on Election Day to prevent intimidation and fraud at the polls. Although officially nonpartisan, the H.B.A. was led and staffed by Fusion enthusiasts—among them the Reverend John Haynes Holmes of the Community Church, who asked for an assignment "to one of the toughest districts, first, because I think I could perhaps be of the best service there, and secondly, because I should value the practical experience of studying conditions in such a place." La Guardia also enjoyed the services of a private corps of commandos who called themselves the Fusioneers. Consisting of Italo-American prizefighters, Ivy League college athletes, and other young men handy with their fists, they served as shock troops for the Honest Ballot Association, flushed out Tammany hoodlums who tried to break up Fusion rallies, and delighted in communicating with their leader in military language.

"Flank attack completely repulsed and battle continues on original front," a Fusioneer commander wired La Guardia after one engagement. "Report received," the Major wired back. "Deploy your forces and continue advance. . . . Heavy barrage will precede you."[16]

A frictionless machine? Hardly. How could it have been when diverse organizations jealously maintained their separate identities and when professional politicians expressed scorn for amateurs and the latter accused the professionals of working secretly for Tammany Hall? And beyond all the suspicion, bickering, and recriminations there was no telling when La Guardia's famous temper would explode. "This"—he dashed off a memo to an aide who had sent him a proposal for tax reform—"is about as asinine, stupid, incoherent nonsensical a collection of stupid suggestions as I have ever seen in all of my years of dealing with damn fool ideas."

"Now, Fiorello," his official campaign manager, William Chadbourne, would murmur on such occasions, "Now, Fiorello. . . ."

Still, it was just the kind of organization that one would expect of a politician who throve on the tumult and confusion of improvisation and all his life had exploited the vitality and looseness of diversity. Like La Guardia himself, his organization must be evaluated by what it did and not by how it looked. It gave him sound advice. It ground out lively publicity. It created a contagious enthusiasm for his cause. It coordinated and harnessed the energies of his motley followers—as the facing chart reveals—in each of the five boroughs down to the election district level. At one Manhattan rally, to cite a random example, La Guardia's managers arranged for him to speak under the auspices of the West Side Italian-American Republican Club, the City Fusion Party of the Seventh Assembly District, the Knickerbocker Democratic Club of the same Assembly District, the Irish-American League for Fusion, and the Master Shoe Repairers' Association.[17]

Both McKee and La Guardia believed that habitual non-voters had it within their power to decide who would be the next mayor. Of an estimated three and a half million New

BOROUGH ORGANIZATION CHART
FUSION CAMPAIGN

Ben Howe
(Director Organization)

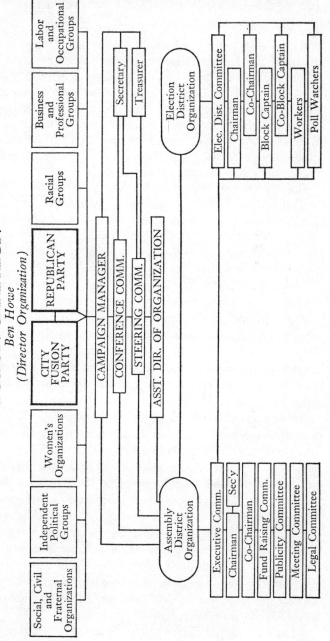

Yorkers eligible to vote, only a million and a half ordinarily bothered to register for municipal elections. McKee entered the race too late (he announced his candidacy eight days before registration week began) to launch a drive of his own. La Guardia's organization, on the other hand, was at full strength by mid-October and co-operated with other anti-Tammany groups to push enrollment up to an unprecedented 2,324,389. At the same time, the Honest Ballot Association and Fusioneers prevented a repetition of fifty thousand fraudulent registrations that Tammany had rung up in 1932.[18]

Only with regard to finances did La Guardia come off second best to McKee, whose campaign received two dollars for every one contributed to Fiorello's. The latter's managers had trouble raising money among wealthy conservative Republicans because, according to Paul Windels, a number of them "feared that our man might be a half-baked socialist."[19] All the same, Fusion's war chest, reported at a little more than a hundred and eighty thousand dollars, was enough to pay for posters, parades, radio appearances, leaflets, and other expenses. La Guardia's army of volunteers worked free, and Depression prices were such that the City Fusion Party rented an entire floor in the Paramount Building for only sixty dollars a month. In 1933, unlike 1929, La Guardia finished the campaign in the black.

What demands explanation, therefore, is not why his budget was smaller than McKee's but why it was larger than when he had run against Walker. He received financial assistance from some big Republican contributors (John D. Rockefeller, Jr., among them) who four years earlier had rejected him as irresponsible. Seabury now stood behind La Guardia and had also proved him right about Tammany in 1929. What is more, La Guardia's campaign caught on, as it had not against Walker, among many voters of modest income who gave according to their means. Finally, some of Fiorello's managers solicited the Italo-American underworld, though without his knowledge according to Ed Corsi, and a few hoodlums came to the aid of Fusion for reasons of ethnic pride.[20]

"The Democrats haven't recognized the Italians," Joe

Adonis is reported to have complained. "There is no reason for the Italians to support anybody but La Guardia. . . ."[21]

But money and registrations, organization and poll watchers, advisors, running mates, and all the rest were important merely as tactical weapons. The battle for office in 1933 was ultimately decided by the combatants themselves, their personalities, their programs, and their policies. What did they say? And to whom, where, and how?

3. On the Stump: Ours Is a Crusade, Not a Political Contest

The La Guardia of 1933 resembled in many respects the La Guardia of 1929. He crisscrossed the city as before, delivering four speeches to each of his opponents' one, and warned New Yorkers that their city was dying from "Tammanyitis." The infection was no less dangerous in its Bronx-Flynn-McKee form, he insisted, than in the Manhattan-Curry-O'Brien syndrome. Once again he campaigned in the slashing style and sartorial unkemptness that were his trademark. He was, as before, the finger-pointing, arm-waving, foot-stomping orator, the familiar Fiorello who traded taunts with hecklers in the audience, the La Guardia of old whose soggy collars and wilted shirts, rumpled jackets, baggy trousers, and ties askew were a source of despair to both his staff and the men's furnishing industry.

"Do not appear in public to speak before anybody unless you are dressed in a suit that has been pressed that day," his Queens manager begged after seeing a newspaper picture of him in disarray.[22]

But his speeches got through to the electorate as they had not in 1929. For one thing, Seabury often accompanied him on the stump, and their duo blended in dramatic political counterpoint. For another, a split-timing schedule arranged by George B. Compton, who was experienced in such things, enabled La Guardia to average a dozen and more appearances a day before groups ranging from the Union League Club to the Italian-American Barbers Association. And thanks to Paul Blanshard, a born muckraker in charge of Fusion's research bureau (in a no-nonsense memo he asked Fiorello not to "refer to this office nuts, cranks, and martyrs, just because they have a kick against the government. Get rid of them yourself to save our time."),[23] La Guardia's speeches rested on the most careful detail. They were also more thoughtful than in 1929. Generalizing about the character of municipal government, which he had failed to do in the Walker campaign, he linked the district leader system to corruption and incompetence as cause and effect.

"Ours is not a political contest," he pleaded in the peroration of his October 2 Cooper Union address. "It is a crusade. We are not fighting against particular candidates. We are fighting against a cruel, vicious political system. We want to wrest control from the political bosses and make our city what we want it to be, a great big, beautiful, kind New York."[24]

For the next five weeks, particularly before merchants, taxpayers, bankers, advertisers, engineers, real estate brokers, and other businessmen, La Guardia elaborated on the theme of municipal purification and municipal rebirth via nonpartisanship. He preached the Good Government gospel of efficiency, honesty, economy, and a balanced budget. A Harvard Club audience heard him declare: "A city, like an individual, cannot borrow itself out of debt." He promised to reform assessment rates; restore the city's credit rating; unify the transit system; and shrink the bureaucracy through a new charter that would eliminate useless jobs held by what he variously called clubhouse loafers and Tammany hacks, tinhorn politicians, crooked oligarchs, and leeches. In contrast to an "army of parasites fattening at the trough of the city treasury," only technicians of proved ability would be retained and recruited for a Fusion administration.

"Municipal government," La Guardia summed up his philosophy in a particularly succinct phrase, "is city housekeeping."[25]

Not only had La Guardia not expressed that point of view four years earlier, but in his 1929 acceptance speech in Mecca Temple he actually had promised G.O.P. district leaders a patronage feast if they got out the vote for him. "I'll see to it," he told them unequivocally, "that you'll be recognized." Four years later, in the same hall before much the same crowd, he warned party workers that training and experience would be the sole requirement for jobs in his administration. "On January 1, when I enter City Hall, I go out of politics for four years," the La Guardia of 1933 proclaimed. The reason? "One can't be a good fellow and a good mayor."[26]

He meant what he said and would later prove it through his appointments. But why the change? Was it because he wanted to revenge himself against Republican leaders for knifing him in 1929 even after he had promised to play the game according to their clubhouse rules? Or was it because McKee was claiming that he, too, stood for government unbossed and graftless, neither Democratic nor Republican, but by qualified personnel administering municipal affairs on sound business principles?

Whatever the reasons for La Guardia's turnabout, his contest with McKee narrowed down to the question of which man could best give New York City a responsible as well as an independent administration. In one of the few epigrams Mc-Kee attempted in the campaign he exclaimed: "I am against a government by fury as I am against a government by Curry." La Guardia he denounced as a dangerous demagogue, and Seabury as the "boss" of Fusion. Fiorello retaliated by reminding the public of what McKee had said on becoming acting mayor in 1932: "I AM AN ORGANIZATION DEMOCRAT, ALWAYS HAVE BEEN AND ALWAYS WILL BE."[27]

But until mid-October, when the campaign turned into a thumb-in-the-eye Donnybrook, it was not La Guardia so much as the men around him who raised questions on the stump about McKee's credentials to lead a crusade against Tammany. He did not represent the New Deal, Professor Berle insisted with the authority of a brain truster, for President Roosevelt "has stated definitely and categorically that he was neutral in this fight." If McKee was not the White House candidate, then who did stand behind him? He was the "pliant, subservient and vacillating tool" of the "adroit and sinister Flynn," charged Seabury, who further accused the Bronx boss of conspiring to take over the Hall so that he could out-Curry Curry and out-Tweed Tweed in plundering the city.[28]

Walter Lippmann, in a superb analysis directed toward the independent voter, cut through the campaign catcalling to isolate the real issue. O'Brien stood for the perpetuation of the old order of municipal mismanagement by semiliterate district leaders, while McKee represented a revolt of the organization's enlightened faction against the benighted wing, and La Guardia was proposing to destroy the system altogether and start afresh. The choice before independents, Lippmann therefore concluded, turned on the following questions:

> Can the machine be sufficiently reformed by men who, until a month ago, were part of it? Or is it desirable to overthrow the whole machine of misgovernment and install men who are entirely unentangled with it? Is New York to wipe the dust off the furniture or sweep out the dirt that is under it? Is it going to trust Mr. McKee to reform the district leaders or is it going to separate those district leaders from treasury and the sources of government power? Do the people wish a partial change of control at the top or a radical change of control from top to bottom? In the McKee faction they have men who have been a part of the existing machine, have done business with it, have acquiesced in it, have sustained it, still represent an important part of it, and, barring miracles, must continue to compromise with it. In Fusion they have a group of candidates who are the sworn enemies of the machine, owe nothing to it, have every interest in destroying it, and no interest in compromising with it.[29]

Lippmann came out for Fiorello and Fusion, and so did the New York *Times, Herald Tribune, World-Telegram,* and *Evening Post.* McKee was backed by Hearst's *Evening Journal* and *American,* the *Daily News* and its *Daily Mirror* tabloid competitor, and the conservative Republican *Sun,* which attacked La Guardia as a radical who only a few years before had bolted the party to run with La Follette on both the Progressive and Socialist tickets. As for O'Brien, perhaps the most forgotten candidate of a major party in modern American history, he would have had no newspaper support at all had it not been for Tammany's own New York *Democrat.*

La Guardia clearly won the battle for the city's most prestigious editorial pages. But the ones for Recovery reached 4,137,792 readers, whereas the combined circulation of newspapers for Fusion added up to only 1,370,953. Such statistics told Fiorello what he already had surmised; namely, that middle-class Good Government reformers favored him and that they constituted a minority of the city's population. Not only were his Paramount Building headquarters staffed by men and women of that sort, but the Citizens Union, the sole mugwump association to endorse candidates, reversed its 1929 rejection of him as a demagogue to pronounce him a responsible leader of an imperative cause.[30]

Yet the crusade for good government scarcely appealed as an end in itself to the other New York congested in the hell's kitchens of each of the five boroughs. By the Depression winter of 1933 there were as many New Yorkers on relief as there were residents in all of Buffalo, and an estimated third of the city's population lived in slums "unfit for human habitation. . . ."[31] The numerous poor sustained the Tammany machine, La Guardia knew from long experience, because the Tammany machine befriended the poor. Favors were exchanged for votes, and if the practice violated the mugwump conscience, both the boss and his constituents thought it only right that politics be immediate, personal, and helpful in time of need.

The task before La Guardia was as clear as it was urgent: to build a bridge between the aspirations of the Goo Goos and the needs of the Disinherited.

He attempted to do so in speeches to trade unionists and social workers, public health authorities and housing reformers, ethnic groups and progressives in general. Before such audiences Fiorello dwelt more on welfare and less on economy. Administrative efficiency, moreover, was not advocated as an end in itself but as a means to change society. Fiorello talked about social justice "feelingly," as he put it, "because I feel so strongly about it." Didn't his first wife and baby daughter die from tuberculosis contracted in lower Manhattan? And as a Congressman from the city's most wretched slums for nearly twenty years had he not perceived that "too often life in New York is merely a squalid succession of days. . . ."?

"What is needed," he implored one audience, "is government with a heart."[32]

La Guardia proposed to take politics out of relief; to restore the city's credit so as to be eligible for Federal public-works grants that would put the unemployed to work; to reform and extend the city's health services; to increase the number of playgrounds; to transform dismal blotches of wasteland into green parks; to provide free legal aid in the courts for New Yorkers who needed it; to clear the slums through tax-supported housing. In effect, he was proposing a local welfare state to replace the Tammany district leader who doled out a Christmas turkey, bucket of coal, or some other form of charity. The poor didn't need charity, La Guardia insisted, they needed to live in a society humanely reformed.

"In putting the substructure of decent environment under life," La Guardia said, "we shall be making the greatest single contribution."[33]

McKee spoke both less often and less convincingly than La Guardia about expanding the welfare functions of municipal government. The reason is that, despite his claim to being a New Dealer, he simply was not the social and economic reformer La Guardia was and had been for a decade and more. Yet not until after the founding of the American Labor Party in 1936, would La Guardia run for election with the support of the progressive wing of organized labor as a bloc. In 1933, apart from Italo-American trade union locals in the clothing industry, the community that rallied most solidly around his welfare program was the community of center and left-of-center intellectuals.

"I am not in politics of any sort, as you know, and my support is private and not worth a damn to you," Roger Baldwin of the American Civil Liberties Union wrote to Fiorello. "But you can't object to a little cheer from the left!"[34]

Numerous others lent their names publicly to La Guardia's cause.* Yet like so many Goo Goos and monied Republicans,

---

* On October 11, 1933, La Guardia was endorsed by—in the language of a Fusion press release—"29 liberal economists, publishers, lawyers, editors, authors, and sociologists." They were, in alphabetical order: Ernest Angell, attorney; Dr. A. A. Berle, attorney and adviser of President Roosevelt; Paul Blanshard, Director of the City Affairs Committee; Heywood Broun, columnist; John O'Hara Cosgrave, painter and illustrator; John Lovejoy Elliott, head of Hudson Guild; John T. Flynn, economist and financial editor of *Collier's;* Walter Frank, lawyer; Carter Goodrich, professor of economics at Columbia University; Ernest Gruening, editor of the *Nation;* Arthur Garfield Hays, attorney for the American Civil Liberties Union; Norman Hapgood, editor; Hubert C. Herring, Social Service Secretary of the Congregational Church; Ira A. Hirschmann, advertising and merchandising expert; B. W. Huebsch,

many an intellectual reversed a position he had taken on La Guardia in 1929. The *Nation's* choice in that year, for example, had been Norman Thomas. Why the switch? One reason was that Thomas was out of the race in 1933, and another that La Guardia was now campaigning as a genuine Fusion leader pledged against dividing the spoils with the Republican bosses. The *Nation* endorsed him, one of its writers summing up the case for him in these words:

"La Guardia, with his social progressivism, could make out of New York a gigantic laboratory for civic reconstruction."[35]

In appealing for support among intellectuals, Republicans, mugwumps, and slum dwellers, La Guardia succeeded not only because he personally touched base in all four groups but also because he actively went after the vote. "The *Nation* surely can do a lot in this campaign," he wrote in late August to publisher Oswald Garrison Villard.[36] Before considering

---

publisher; Paul Kellogg, editor of *Survey;* Joseph Wood Krutch, dramatic critic and publicist; Agnes Brown Leach, of the League of Women Voters; Bishop F. J. McConnell, former president of the Federal Council of Churches; Professor Parker T. Moon of Columbia; Amos Pinchot, lawyer and publicist; Walter H. Pollak, lawyer; Mary K. Simkhovitch, head of Greenwich House; Carl Van Doren, author and head of the Literary Guild; Oswald Garrison Villard, publisher of the *Nation;* Lillian Wald, former head of the Henry Street Settlement; Helen Woodward, author; William E. Woodward, author; and Will Irwin, novelist. A week and half later, Fusion announced the names of "one hundred and three deans and leading professors of government, law, and economics in all the universities in New York City" who were supporting La Guardia and the ticket he was heading. The most prominent of these included Dean Young B. Smith, of the Columbia University Law School; Dean Frank Somer, of the New York University Law School; Dean Archibald A. Bouton, of the College of Arts and Sciences at New York University; Dr. Charles Cheney Hyde, a world figure in the field of international law; Professor Russell Forbes, Director of the Division of Research in Public Administration at N.Y.U.; Dr. E. George Payne, Assistant Dean of the School of Education at N.Y.U.; Professor Horace Kallen, Professor Joseph D. McGoldrick of Columbia; Dean Joseph W. Barker, of the Columbia School of Engineering; and Professor Philip Owen Badger, Assistant Chancellor of New York University. Among those who earlier had made public their endorsement were: Nicholas Murray Butler, president of Columbia; Dean Virginia Gildersleeve of Barnard and Dean Edward Lee McBain of Columbia. As La Guardia's correspondence reveals, he also received the support of the following writers: Henry F. Pringle, Harry Elmer Barnes, Theodore Dreiser, and Hendrik Willem van Loon.

the extent to which La Guardia's coalition held together on Election Day we must first consider still another element in it, the ethnic vote; for in courting that vote La Guardia, and his opponents as well, released the least rational issue of the campaign: anti-Semitism.

4. Climax, Thumb-in-the-Eye Style

The melting pot was boiling in 1933 as never before since World War I. Hitler's rise to power had intensified the self-consciousness not only of Jewish-Americans but of German-Americans as well. Negroes were groping under the impact of the Depression for a new political identity after years of subservience to the Republican Party. For those Irish who were ashamed of Tammany Hall ("You are a better and nobler Irishman than Mayor O'Brien," wrote one Celt to Fiorello), there were still others who shared the fear expressed by Ed Flynn that their kind might "lose an equal place in the sun . . . which other races in this city enjoy."

Italo-Americans on the other hand were resentful that they were close to the bottom economically and socially and had not received political recognition in proportion to their numbers. The best index to their hurt and therefore aggressive pride was how their newspapers indiscriminately celebrated no matter which Latin achievement: Primo Carnera's knocking out Jack Sharkey for the world's heavyweight championship, General Italo Balbo's record air flight from Italy to Chicago and back, Tony Canzoneri's impending lightweight title bout with Barney Ross, Benito Mussolini's "genius," and F. H. La Guardia's quest for the mayoralty in the biggest Latin city in the world. But the more the colony indulged in self-congratulations, the more it betrayed feelings of inferiority. More than any other ancestral group in New York City, Italo-Americans were determined to seize an equal place in the sun.[37]

Each of the three candidates played tribal politics, boasting of his immigrant parents and singing hymns to the marvels of the melting pot. "We Irish, Italians, Jews," is how O'Brien might begin a speech in which he described the prejudice he had encountered as a boy growing up in Yankee New England. But La Guardia was an older hand at the game, commanded more languages than either of his opponents, and enjoyed the services of former U. S. Commissioner of Immigration and Naturalization Ed Corsi in going after the ethnic vote. There was scarcely a group that Corsi, head of Fusion's foreign language division, did not organize or have organized into a committee for La Guardia. To list all the endorsements would be tedious, and it is enough to say that they covered so broad a spectrum as the Norse Republican League of America and Harlem's *Amsterdam News;* the Turkish Aid Society and Syrian-American Citizens Committee; *Il Progresso,* the Hungarian League of New York City, *Jewish Morning Journal,* Croatian-Americans for Fusion, and on and on.[38]

La Guardia might appeal to an audience to vote for him in words as direct as these: "I promise a clean, honest, efficient municipal government which will take into consideration the wants and interests of the Porto Rican people."

Or he could break in unannounced in the middle of a religious service in Harlem and cry out: "Peace, Father Divine, peace be with you all! I say, Father Divine, no matter what you want, I will support you. I am going to clean up this city." But not a one of the five thousand worshipers seemed to know who he was. "No! No!" the crowd shouted, "Father" was going to clean up the city and no one else. So La Guardia tried again: "And I come here tonight to ask Father Divine's help and counsel." This time the saints approved: "Wonderful—Peace—Amen." He departed as quickly as he had arrived, leaving the congregation singing:

> Father, I surrender,
> Father, I surrender
> All . . .[39]

Robert Moses has written "that in exploiting racial and religious prejudices La Guardia could run circles around the bosses he despised and derided. When it came to raking ashes of Old World hates, warming ancient grudges, waving the bloody shirt, tuning the ear to ancestral voices, he could easily outdemagogue the demagogues. And for what purpose? To redress old wrongs abroad? To combat foreign levy or malice domestic? To produce peace on the Danube, the Nile, the Jordan? Not on your tintype. Fiorello La Guardia knew better. He knew that the aim of the rabble rousers is simply to shoo into office for entirely extraneous, illogical and even silly reasons the municipal officials who clean city streets, teach in schools, protect, house and keep healthy, strong and happy millions of people crowded together here."[40]

But if La Guardia's ends were justified, the means were particularly dangerous in the overheated atmosphere of 1933. For every Jewish friend for Fusion he won by attacking Hitler, Fiorello antagonized at least one Nazi fellow traveler. "A million or more Americans of German descent," one of them wrote to him, "will show you on Election Day that a little and conceited Italian cannot insult the great German people unpunished. They will leave you alone with your Jews. . . ."[41] The line between pride and prejudice was a thin one, and in making race, religion, and nationality a part of the campaign La Guardia, and his opponents as well, prompted the bigots to speak up. One Fascist sent Fiorello the following:

Major La Guardia
City.

Sir:

As long as you associate
with JEWS
you are an enemy of the American people.
We do not want Jews.
We hate Jews.
We hate you, if you are with the Jews.
The Jew is America's downfall.
The Jew is to blame for our troubles.

We We We We We We We We We We We We We We
Hate
Hate
Hate Hate Hate Hate Hate Hate Hate Hate
Jews
Jews
Jews
Jews
Jews

Viva Italia   Down with the Jew.

No Jew for America.

La Guardia ignored such diatribes as emanating from a diseased mind on a fringe both too far out and too small to affect the outcome of the election. It was something else, however, when in mid-October La Guardia called attention to an article that McKee had written in 1915 as a high-school teacher questioning the moral and political reliability of New York City's Jewish youth. The Jews constituted a little more than a fourth of the electorate.

This most sensational part of the campaign derived from McKee's attempt to identify himself with Governor Lehman as well as with President Roosevelt. Seabury had been making speeches against Lehman for not prosecuting the Tammany district leaders dirtied by the 1930–1932 investigations, and some of McKee's supporters insinuated that the attack sprang from anti-Semitism. The insinuation was false, but knowing that Lehman was the idol of the Jewish electorate, La Guardia implored Seabury to turn to another target. Seabury refused and La Guardia was on the point of disavowing his criticism when Paul Windels talked him out of it, explaining that a rupture between the Little Flower and the Mayflower could only benefit Recovery.

McKee tried to force that rupture in a telegram to La Guardia demanding that he repudiate Seabury's "base and reckless slander" of a noble man and dedicated public servant. "See!" La Guardia exclaimed to Windels, "I told you something like this would happen. I should have disavowed Seabury's speeches a couple of days ago."

On the contrary, Windels replied. Ever since the Flynn-Farley-Roosevelt conference in September, Fusion had been keeping McKee's 1915 article in reserve should it be necessary to use against him. "Here is the opportunity," Windels said to La Guardia, "to put McKee's own record right up to him." That is precisely what they did. A stenographer was summoned, and La Guardia's counter-thrust to McKee's maneuver escalated the struggle over the Jewish vote.[42]

"Are you trying to draw a red herring across the cowardly, contemptible and unjust attack that you have made and published against a great race so gloriously represented by our governor?" La Guardia wired back. "Answer that, Mr. McKee, and think twice before you send me another telegram."[43] The newspapers not only ran La Guardia's reply but republished McKee's "A Serious Question" of 1915.

The primary purpose of the controversial article, which appeared in the *Catholic World*, was to urge Catholic families to support the New York City public high-school system in larger numbers than they were doing. In the course of making his plea McKee claimed that there were three Jewish high-school students for every Christian, and that "in overwhelming numbers" they were abandoning Judaism, embracing Godless socialism, and defending lying and cheating in the materialist pursuit of money. "Surely we cannot look for ideal results from such material," the twenty-six-year-old educator warned. Yet "it is to such as these, that our [Catholic] children, who are without the benefits of education, must bow in later years."[44]

Those words sounded especially ominous in 1933, and Samuel Untermyer, a lawyer high in Democratic circles who had been supporting McKee, denounced them as a "reverberation of Hitlerism."[45]

McKee was stunned by the turn of events and hurried into conference with his managers. One of them suggested that the attack be ignored, and another that a whispering campaign be started against La Guardia. McKee decided to meet the charge of anti-Semitism head on. In a major radio address he protested that his 1915 words had been torn out of context. Reading from a paragraph in his article commending Jews for their pursuit of education and as "excellent students and often profound scholars," he insisted: "I did not criticize Jews or Judaism. I criticized only those Jews who abandoned Judaism. Do Jews do less?"[46]

Untermyer, saying that he was willing to forgive and forget a youthful indiscretion, expressed astonishment that McKee should choose to defend his sentiments of twenty years before. "Mr. McKee's explanation," he snapped in a statement to the press, "explains nothing." La Guardia agreed and added: "McKee ought to be twice ashamed of himself."

But many of McKee's Jewish neighbors in the Bronx and former students, along with such well-known leaders as Rabbi

Jonah B. Wise, Henry Morgenthau, Sr., Nathan Straus, Jr., and Judge Irving Lehman, testified to his friendship with Jews and sympathy for Jewish institutions and causes. In a letter to the New York *Times* one orthodox believer attacked McKee's detractors as enemies of God and Judaism. More important, the *American Hebrew* reminded the electorate that the 1915 article had been resurrected in the 1925 campaign and that Jews had then given McKee a clean bill of health. "To dig it up now," that journal protested, "is a contemptible attempt to drag the anti-Semitic herring across the trail of paramount local, civic issues that should dominate the campaign."[47]

Even now, although removed by some thirty years from the passion and partisanship of events, one is hard put to say whether La Guardia did a contemptible thing or whether McKee got what he deserved. The crucial question is, Was McKee anti-Semitic? The answer depends on one's definition of anti-Semitism, the context in which McKee wrote his article, and the difference, if any, between the high-school teacher of 1915 and the Recovery Party candidate of 1933.

There is no way of softening his harsh portrait of Jewish students, but his hostility derived from a larger antagonism that he felt toward secularism, socialism, and materialism in general. In 1915 a very conservative Catholic, McKee was offended by so-called modernist heresies of nearly every kind. In other articles for the *Catholic World* his targets ranged from "the license of Luther" to the permissiveness of progressive education, from "pernicious" Jean Jacques Rousseau to the encroaching expansion of the state and such "destroyers" of the family as "the mad desire" for woman suffrage and birth control.[48] If style suggests the man, then McKee revealed himself during World War I as a parochial, self-righteous, militant, and stuffy young pedant who believed that truth was fixed once and for all and that he and his church alone possessed it.* In the 1920's, on the Board of Aldermen, he would earn the sobriquet of "Holy Joe."

* In an article for the *Catholic World* on Catholics in the American Revolution, McKee rhapsodized: "By Catholic daring and enterprise, America was discovered; by Catholic explorers its realms were traversed and its wealth and beauty pictured to the world; by Jesuit missionaries

But even if he had disliked Jews as Jews in 1915, which is by
no means clear, McKee, according to reliable testimony, was
no anti-Semite in 1933. To insinuate that he was, as La Guardia
did, was to be unfair because it was untrue. Yet, without
absolving Fiorello, one must add that Holy Joe also flung
buckets of mud.

Claiming that he would "be an American Mayor and not a
Moscow Mayor," he called La Guardia "a Communist at
heart." The defamation was all the more ridiculous and reckless when he further accused La Guardia of being party to a
G.O.P. cabal to capture City Hall so as to swing New York
behind a Republican candidate against Roosevelt in 1936.[49]
Above all, in trying to force La Guardia to sacrifice either
Seabury or the Jewish vote, McKee made the first nasty feint
that led to the injection of bigotry into the campaign. No
more than the Little Flower did Holy Joe regard the Marquess
of Queensbury rules as relevant to electoral combat. Both men
struck low blows. Each hurled charges at the other so scurrilous and irrelevant and preposterous that an association
should have been founded then and there to protect the
combatants from being fouled and the electorate from being
gulled.

The effects of the Jewish issue on the actual returns will be
discussed in the following chapter. Here it is relevant to note
that La Guardia destroyed whatever chances McKee may have
had to ride into City Hall with a push from the White House.
Back in September, according to Flynn and Farley, the President had promised to invite the Recovery candidate to Washington as an unofficial sign of his approval. The invitation
failed to materialize after La Guardia accused McKee of being
anti-Semitic, despite Flynn's urgent SOS to Roosevelt that his
intervention was all the more necessary to reinstate McKee
with Jewish voters.[50] La Guardia's tactic had isolated his
opponent from the powerful Democratic administration.

McKee appealed to Al Smith for an endorsement and was

---

the light of Christ was first brought to its shores, and by Catholic sub-
jects its first colony was founded. Now by Catholic help [in the Revolu-
tion] a glorious nation was established on its shores." CVI (October,
1917), 89.

turned down. Smith supported no candidate in 1933, but several men formerly associated with the once popular Democratic governor took part in the campaign on either the Fusion or Recovery side. The best-known of them, Robert Moses, joined the La Guardia camp.

"You have no strings on you," the future park commissioner wrote to the future mayor on October 25. "You will owe nothing to Washington and to Albany. You are not engaged in an obscure struggle for the control of a rotten political machine." More, he went on to say that "the Great Statesman McKee is a synthetic character, which never actually existed on sea or land, puffed up by the press a year ago, and now in the process of deflation." What most disturbed Moses was that "McKee is, and always will be, a creature of Mr. Farley and Mr. Flynn. Add New York City to the present political fields of these bosses," Moses concluded, "and we shall have the most ruthless political and patronage machine this country has ever seen, and one with exceedingly low standards."

La Guardia of course released Moses's letter to the press.

All but forgotten, O'Brien was the gentlest campaigner of the three major candidates. But in an election that had taken on aspects of a contest in character assassination, it was predictable that his Tammany managers would feel in their element. One of their typical anti-La Guardia leaflets had this title: *No Red, No Clown Shall Rule This Town.* Fiorello's staid and conservative Republican backers rushed to his aid, but the most effective rebuttal emanated from the Marxist left. The Socialist Party denounced him as an opportunist, the Socialist Labor Party as an instrument for "the ruling class magicians," and the Communist Party as a "capable and valuable servant of finance capital" and "a dangerous foe of the American working class."[51]

To say that La Guardia actually enjoyed the brickbats would be too much, but he was a good deal more stoical about them than some of his inexperienced running mates. "I appreciate what you say about the course that the campaign has taken lately," he wrote on October 30 to a disturbed Fusionist, but "incidents such as occurred in the last few days inevitably creep into any campaign and cannot be avoided."[52]

He brought the election back to the original issue of non-partisan government in a speech at a climactic rally staged in Madison Square Garden on November 2. Preceded by torch-light parades starting from a dozen parts of the city and converging on the Garden after dark, it was the largest and liveliest political demonstration in years, testifying both to the theatrical expertise of La Guardia's organization and the enthusiasm he himself had generated for Fusion. When he entered the arena, at 10:25 P.M., the band struck up his campaign song (it was sung to the tune of "In the Halls of Montezuma") and an ovation broke out that lasted for ten minutes until chairman C. C. Burlingham raised a sign over his head announcing that La Guardia was about to go on the radio.

"My friends, thousands of people came here tonight," he shouted jubilantly into the microphone. "Do you know what that means?"

"Victory!" roared the crowd.[53]

5. *The First Tuesday in November*

There is no way of reconstructing Election Day of 1933 without evoking images of a cops and robbers movie, for the truth about that first Tuesday in November is that it ended with drawn guns.

At around eleven o'clock that night La Guardia burst into the huge room on the top floor of police headquarters where Tammany-appointed employees of the Board of Elections were tabulating the returns. The Mayor-elect's entry was unannounced and unexpected, but he was very quickly recognized, and inspectors, captains, lieutenants, and so on down the line fell over each other to congratulate their new commander-in-chief. He had not come to collect huzzahs. The results in the comptroller's race were being held up from 400 election districts, and La Guardia had rushed over from his own victory celebration at the Paramount Building to prevent the election from being stolen from J. Arthur Cunningham.

"I want four hundred patrolmen mobilized behind headquarters just as fast as they can get here," La Guardia snapped to one police officer. "Get me four hundred patrol wagons," he commanded another, and "roll 'em into the alley behind headquarters as fast as God will let you." The floor was in bedlam as the diminutive chief executive rapped out one order after another. "As fast as each patrolman gets here," he went on, "send 'em to one of the four hundred precincts in which the count for comptroller is being held up. Tell 'em to mount guard over that voting machine with drawn gun."[54]

The irony of that scene and others of November 7 must have seemed delicious to the cynics and scoffers and outright enemies of popular government. Here was the biggest city in the world's oldest republic going through the secular but sacred democratic ritual of changing the guard. The procedure was supposed to be peaceful and orderly, yet the turbulence, the intimidation, the trickery, and the violence were almost beyond belief.

The electoral process had been punctuated throughout the day by arguments, threats, fist fights, black eyes, cracked heads, arrests, and one reported stabbing. Tammany's strength lay in the slums, and it was there that worthies of the Dutch Schultz mob, and other mobs enjoying the Hall's protection, flexed their muscles for the party in power. In one district alone, Boss Al Marinelli's south of Washington Square, some two hundred of the underworld gentry descended on the polling places wearing identical pearl-gray fedoras, shod in hobnailed shoes, and wielding such unhidden dissuaders as brass knuckles, lead pipes, and blackjacks.[55]

It was against such as these that the former World War I Army officer called up the Fusioneers and Honest Ballot Association. Whether Joe Adonis and his boys added brute strength on Election Day to the money they had contributed to Fiorello's cause during the campaign is unknown.[56] La Guardia's two contingents, with manpower equal to that of seven infantry regiments, outnumbered by far Tammany's goon squads and acquitted themselves well under fire. That in 1933 a record number of New Yorkers voted in a municipal election from even the dangerous districts was due in part to the protective shield thrown up by the Little Flower's poll watchers.

He himself stormed into the toughest precincts, usually

accompanied by his wife, a staff member, and representatives of the press. At a public school on East One Hundred and Thirteenth Street between Second and Third Avenues, to cite a single instance, he shouldered his way through a crowd and bore down on a huge man wearing a Tammany badge. "You're a thug," he snapped as he tore the badge from the man's coat. "Now get out of here and keep away." He then turned on a dozen or so others in the crowd and shouted in his screaming soprano: "I know you. You're thugs. You get out of here and keep moving."

Later he said to an aide, "Walter, these fellows are yellow. They're a lot of punks, and I'm going to run them out of the city."[57]

His mood changed to one of serenity early that evening as he received the election returns with Seabury in the quiet elegance of the latter's home. By midevening La Guardia's lead soared over the 200,000 mark. McKee was being overwhelmed in his own Bronx, and Tammany's formerly impregnable Manhattan fief was falling to Fiorello. The crusade was over except for the final and official count.

La Guardia departed for his Paramount Building headquarters, arriving at ten o'clock, and entered the building behind a flying wedge formed by the police. In the ballroom, however, the crush of joyous admirers almost sent the hero to the hospital on the evening of his greatest triumph. Meanwhile, outside in Times Square, a huge crowd tied up traffic for blocks around as they waited for a glimpse of the pint-sized Tammany killer. He climbed out on the marquee of the Paramount Theater to address them. They saw his lips move, but the din drowned out the sound of his voice.

McKee didn't bother to show up at Recovery headquarters, but wild bulls and elephants couldn't keep O'Brien away from the Wigwam on East Seventeenth Street and Fourth Avenue. He assembled with the sachems in the auditorium on the top floor at 9:00 P.M., and for the next two hours sat mostly in silence beside John Curry at a long table in the front of the room. As the clock ticked on and he fell further and further behind McKee as well as La Guardia, Tammany women in the audience were heard to murmur: "It's a shame. A shame. . . . It's a pity, the old dear." At eleven o'clock a slip of paper was laid on the table between the boss and the mayor: the tide was irreversible; Tammany was going under for the first time in twenty years. O'Brien wrote a message of congratulations to La Guardia, then said to reporters: "The man who takes over the City Hall now will have an easier job. . . . I ironed out the worst problems."

The final tally? La Guardia received 868,522 votes to Mc-Kee's 609,053 and O'Brien's 586,672.[58]

The telegrams, radiograms, post cards, and letters that La Guardia received are now filed in bulging folders in the municipal archives and would fill a very thick book if published. Here and there a semiliterate scribbled the drivel that he hated kikes and dagoes and was moving out of New York City because there would be "a influx of wops with Picks and Shovel at city Hall—every day. . . ." At the other extreme a religious fanatic from New Jersey exclaimed: "Daniel come to judgment!!!!! Hurrah for La Guardia, New York's El Duce!!" Far more representative of Fiorello's mail were the following:

May I add my congratulations to those of the countless others who chose your leadership yesterday?

A Banker

We Progressives with Roosevelt and again with you join onward.

Two New Dealers

I pray to God every night for you.

Twelve-Year-Old Boy from Saint Patrick's School

Inebriated by our overwhelming victory you prince of Italo-Americans.

An Italo-American Family

"New Tribune" congratulates you on your overwhelming victory which brings honest government to our great city.

Greek-American Newspaper

Glorious victory. . . . Proud of our blood in your veins. . . .
We acclaim you with our hearty Zivio.

> Croatian-American Fusion
> Committee

A good fighter always wins. Primo's [Carnera] fights are easy
in comparison. He has one enemy only and always in front.
You fought all of them from all directions and won.

> Primo Carnera's Manager

Congratulations to my beloved pupil, the brilliant boy who has
proved father to the man.

> Prescott, Arizona, Teacher[59]

When asked on the day after the election who his appointees would be, La Guardia replied that it was too early to
say, then added with a sly grin: "We may have a literacy test
for some."[60] Soon after, he took a cruise to Panama with Mrs.
La Guardia and friends for a much-needed rest. Contrary to
his public image as a constitutionally inexhaustible bruiser, the
Little Flower's capacity for hard work was more a matter of
will than physique. By the end of the campaign he was very
tired indeed.

V

A Crazy-Quilt Coalition

La Guardia outdistanced each of his opponents in nearly every part of the city. He won all five boroughs, losing only thirteen of the sixty-two assembly districts to O'Brien and a mere three to McKee, and carried a majority of his running mates into the Board of Estimate on the strength of his more than a quarter of a million margin. Impressive in itself, that margin also constituted a stunning comeback after a disastrous defeat to Jimmy Walker only four years before by close to five hundred thousand votes. Even the opposition press wrote that La Guardia had received a strong mandate.

Yet, the press to the contrary and his stunning comeback notwithstanding, La Guardia failed to create a clear-cut political realignment. That achievement would have to wait until the 1937 election. The Democrats, which is to say the feuding Curry and Flynn factions, controlled the city-wide Board of Aldermen, the Bronx and Manhattan borough presidencies, the New York County district attorney's office, and all other county offices high and low. Furthermore, between them McKee and O'Brien piled up 327,203 more votes than La Guardia. Their return must be considered a joint Democratic return, for few New Yorkers had accepted Ed Flynn's man as a nonpartisan candidate. Despite the Little Flower's political coloration, New York City was still a Democratic town in 1933.

La Guardia had of course made it less so, but no one understood better than he that his work had just begun to bring a majority of the people round to his philosophy of government. He received 40.37 per cent of the vote to McKee's 28.31 per cent and O'Brien's 27.27 per cent, with the remainder going to the Socialist, Communist, Socialist Labor, and three other minor party candidates. What all this boils down to is that La Guardia's mandate came from only two out of five voters. That minority was smaller than first meets the eye, for if one includes in the electoral equation the more than a million New Yorkers who had the right to vote but didn't bother to register, the sum of La Guardia's mandate added up to a mere 23.77 per cent of the *eligible* electorate.[1]

That statistic alone is enough to puncture the legend that in 1933 a city united in full force against a corrupt political machine to sweep the reforming Little Flower into office. Other statistics to be presented shortly will demonstrate, furthermore, that tens of thousands of voters for La Guardia were scarcely interested in reform at all. If election statistics are being emphasized in this analysis, it is because they are indispensable for grasping the character of La Guardia's mandate. Only by breaking them down by precincts can we discover who voted for him and why.

Given the fantastic human variety in the city's almost four thousand election districts, and Fiorello's celebrated genius for transcending differences, it was predictable that he would be a rallying point for a crazy-quilt coalition. Fully to describe it would require a hundred tongues, for ethnically it ranged from Anglo-Saxon to Sicilian, socially from Park Avenue to Harlem, philosophically from Marxist to Fascist, religiously from Unitarian to Eastern Orthodox, and economically from Wall Street to Union Square. Yet, one can say that in political terms it consisted essentially of three kinds of New Yorkers: regular Republicans, dissident Democrats, and independent Socialists.

To understand the meaning of his mandate we must examine his appeal to each of the three, and since he was a Republican let us start with the Republicans.

1. *Hoover, Yes, La Guardia, Yes*

That the American votes as an individual for candidates whom he thinks will best promote the public good cannot be denied. Yet as early as the eighteenth century no less an authority than James Madison observed that the individual tends to see the public good through the lenses of his own parochial interests. Today there is general agreement that most men and and women approach the ballot box with predispositions deriving from party habit, income, social status, religion, and ancestry.[2]

By such criteria New York City was, as La Guardia recognized only too well, a Republican's nightmare in the fourth decade of the twentieth century.

The census taker of 1930 broke down the city's population of 6,930,446 persons into one-twentieth Negro, one-fifth native white of native parentage, one-third foreign born, and two-fifths second-generation American. For every four New Yorkers, in other words, only one was not an immigrant or the child of immigrants. The median family expenditure for 1930 stood just above three thousand dollars (by the Depression year of 1933 it must have dropped considerably), and only one in six families lived in a single-family home of its own. As for religious affiliation, the Federal Government took no census of it, but the leading authority of that day, Dr. Walter Laidlaw, calculated that New York City was 36.9 per cent Protestant, 34.1 per cent Catholic, 27.1 per cent Jewish, 1.7 per cent Eastern Orthodox, and a fraction unclassified.[3]

None of this contained the human stuff by which Republicans were mass produced, and by the 1930's the Grand Old Party seemed irrevocably to have lost the battle of the census returns. Of 2,324,389 enrolled New York City voters in 1933, only 435,966 were registered Republicans. Appealing to only 20 per cent of the electorate in Italian East Harlem, 30 per cent in mixed Italian-Scandinavian Bay Ridge, 40 per cent in Negro Harlem and Bedford, and 45 per cent in Jewish precincts of Central Park West, the Republican Party was a coalition party of minorities largely drawn from within minorities. Only among the dwindling number of middle-class to wealthy white Anglo-Saxon Protestants did a majority of Republican voters exist.[4]

The point of all this is that La Guardia, who ran in both the Republican and City Fusion columns, was seeking office when his party had sunk to an historical low in popularity. Never amounting to much on the municipal level, its Presidential candidates had nevertheless carried New York City since the first Abraham Lincoln campaign of 1860. Al Smith shattered the succession in 1928; and four years later F.D.R. repeated the Happy Warrior's romp over Herbert Hoover in Greater New York, winning by an almost three-to-one margin of 1,455,176 to 584,056 votes.[5] Since then no Republican candidate for President, not even the charismatic war hero who entered the White House in 1952, has triumphed in the Empire State south of the Westchester County line.

But in 1933, with the Democratic electorate split in two and La Guardia needing a mere 750,000 votes or so to win, close to half a million registered Republicans had it within their power to decide whether he would be the next mayor of New York City. It would seem that they furnished him more than his margin of victory, for almost half of his 868,522 total from the Republican and City Fusion parties was recorded in the G.O.P. line.[6] However, since many a Democrat voted for him in that line and many a Republican pulled down the lever for him over the City Fusion Party emblem, the return in the Republican column is an unreliable measure of La Guardia's Republican support. A more reliable way of estimating it is to compare the results of the mayoralty contest of 1933 with those of the Presidential election of the previous year.

Such a comparison indicates that La Guardia received the bulk of the vote cast for the Republican Hoover in 1932. In only seven assembly districts, for example, did Hoover score 40 per cent or better (his city-wide average was 27 per cent), and La Guardia's return from those exceptionally strong (for New York) Republican areas of the city added up to an average identical to Hoover's 44 per cent. Another way of describing the correlation between 1932 and 1933 is by the following formula: wherever the Democratic Roosevelt had run low, La Guardia ran on average as high as had his fellow Republican Hoover.

ONLY DISTRICTS IN WHICH HOOVER GOT
40 PER CENT OR MORE OF THE VOTE[7]

Assembly District	Hoover 1928	Hoover 1932	La Guardia 1933
Negro Districts			
Manhattan's 21st: Harlem	55.26	42.05	39.60
Brooklyn's 17th: Bedford	48.81	39.95	42.57
Silk Stocking Districts			
Manhattan's 10th	48.23	43.05	51.43
Manhattan's 15th	54.98	53.87	47.63
Suburban Districts			
Brooklyn's 21st: Flatbush	48.46	42.34	46.74
Queens' 6th: Flushing-Jamaica East	54.72	42.29	38.26
Queens' 4th: Forest Hills	54.77	42.73	42.71
AVERAGE	52.17	43.75	44.13
CITY-WIDE AVERAGE	36.71	26.62	40.37

Here is how the high-low formula operated in the last
G.O.P. stronghold in the city. Manhattan's predominantly
Anglo-Saxon Protestant Fifteenth Assembly District was the
only one in Greater New York that Hoover had carried
against Roosevelt in 1932, and a year later La Guardia pene-
trated even the inner ring along Central Park East and South
to take every gut Republican precinct but one. That some
voters cut him is clear—he fell 6 percentage points below
Hoover's 54 per cent—but La Guardia's district-wide return
of 48 per cent was so good (it was 11 per cent better than his
Manhattan average) that with McKee and O'Brien killing each
other off he trounced his closest rival in the Fifteenth by a 17
per cent margin.

This pattern—Republicans remaining loyal to La Guardia
and Democrats dividing their vote between McKee and
O'Brien—repeated itself in another silk stocking district and in
two Negro and three suburban districts. The table above
shows in detail how, in 1933, the pattern worked to the Republican La Guardia's advantage in the seven assembly districts
that had been most resistant to Roosevelt's Democratic appeal
in 1932 (and to Al Smith's before him in 1928).

The Tenth deserves special comment, for it was the sole assembly district in Manhattan in addition to East Harlem's normally Democratic Italo-American Eighteenth and Twentieth that La Guardia swept by a majority. A huge area extending from south of Washington Square to just below Central Park between Lexington and Seventh (at one point, Eighth) Avenues, it contained the garment industry, the theater district, the city's two railroad terminals, the largest department stores, and numerous clubs, restaurants, hotels, and other commercial establishments. Tenement house districts backed up on elegant residential neighborhoods, and the seamier neighborhoods around Pennsylvania Station, off Times Square, and in Greenwich Village and Chelsea housed a significant portion of the borough's poor and foreign-born. Their votes, particularly those of Italo-American Democrats in the southern part of the Tenth, enabled La Guardia to do better than Hoover and clear the 50 per cent mark.

But that push succeeded because Fiorello received sturdy support from another voting bloc. Only the Fifteenth Assembly District immediately to the north exceeded the Tenth in its concentration of New York City's wealthiest Anglo-Saxon families. Living on or off lower Fifth Avenue, in the Gramercy Park and Murray Hill sections, or along the midtown Park Avenue–Madison Avenue gold coast, the majority of those families would no sooner give up their Republican identity than their Protestant affiliation.

That is largely why Republicans who declared for Hoover in 1932 also declared for La Guardia in 1933. Most people vote for their party's choice except under the most unusual circumstances, and in 1933 the character of the campaign and of La Guardia's opponents was working for Fiorello. None but the most whimsical G.O.P. type could be attracted to O'Brien. The clean-cut McKee, a banker and a conservative, was more appealing and cut into Fiorello's Republican return. But La Guardia was more appealing still. McKee was not only a Democrat but the most dangerous specimen of the breed: a candidate first proposed by That Man in the White House. In the end there was no one to turn to but La Guardia. However crude and unreliable, he stood well with such party leaders as Macy and Mellen and could be counted on to destroy the local Democracy if given the chance.

What is more, his conception of good government fitted into Republican doctrine. His program of efficiency, honesty, and fiscal responsibility sounded orthodox enough to the independent businessmen, downtown lawyers, bankers, brokers, corporation executives, homeowners, and suburbanites who formed the backbone of New York City's Grand Old Party. As for La Guardia's social welfare planks, they were not based on radical principles but rather harmonized with Herbert Hoover's credo that the responsibility for coping with social problems lay with local government. On that much liberal Republicans like Newbold Morris and conservative Republicans like Kingsland Macy agreed.

"I cannot understand—" a Park Avenue veteran of the La Guardia coalition was reminiscing in 1956—"why it is so hard for people today to believe that Republicans like myself supported Fiorello. Sure, we were afraid that he might be a bit too radical. But he promised to clean up the city, throw out Tammany, and run things on sound business principles. That was something a conservative could vote for."[8]

The over-all Hoover Republican vote for La Guardia fell probably between 450,000 and 500,000[9] and gave him a solid base on which to build a victorious coalition. McKee and O'Brien, on the other hand, not only cut into each other but together ran 260,451 ballots behind Roosevelt. Therein lies the most significant part of the swing vote of 1933. Who among the Democrats were jarred loose from party loyalty and kicked over the traces to rally behind the Fusion standard bearer for mayor? To answer that question we again have to compare the 1932 and 1933 elections.

2. *Roosevelt, Yes, La Guardia, Yes, and Mussolini and Marinelli, Too.*

There were thirty-four assembly districts in which Roosevelt exceeded his 67 per cent sweep of the city as a whole, and in twelve of them La Guardia not only topped his own 40 per cent city-wide tally but actually averaged more votes than did O'Brien and McKee *combined*. That he did so was obviously due to a massive desertion from the Democratic Party. O'Brien plummeted as much as 50 percentage points under Roosevelt, whereas La Guardia tripled Hoover's return. Below, in a comparison (by percentages) of the 1932 and 1933 election results in the twelve districts in question, is a rough measure of the Democratic defection to La Guardia.

Who were the Democrats who bolted their party for La Guardia? All but Brooklyn's Sixteenth (to be discussed later) were covered by what the Department of Health called "sore spots," of which the symptoms and causes were high density of population, low income, substandard housing, abnormal incidence of disease, and appalling rates of infant mortality. In

DEMOCRATIC DEFECTIONS

PRESIDENTIAL ELECTION: 1932

Assembly District	Roosevelt	Hoover	Norman Thomas (Socialist)
Manhattan	%	%	%
2 Greenwich Village	86.30	10.96	1.84
18 Lower East Harlem	74.88	21.07	2.75
20 Upper East Harlem	75.66	19.99	2.91
Bronx			
6 East Bronx	71.70	21.37	6.25
7 Tremont	72.41	12.90	9.72
Brooklyn			
4 Navy Yard	77.33	15.61	5.50
6 Stuyvesant	69.88	18.44	9.35
8 Gowanus	83.71	14.35	1.34
13 Bushwick	81.64	13.50	3.58
16 Bensonhurst, Gravesend, Borough Park, Seagate	73.18	14.42	9.75
19 Bushwick	79.38	14.34	4.68
23 Brownsville	72.42	13.98	9.67
AVERAGE	76.54	15.91	5.64
AVERAGE FOR CITY	66.32	26.62	5.58

plainer language, the areas with the largest numbers of Democrats for La Guardia were, or contained, slums and near slums inhabited by the poor and even the poorest of New York City's poor.[10]

But unlike Roosevelt, La Guardia did not win the whole of the normally monolithic Democratic slum vote. He won the Italo-American slum vote. A substantial number of Italians lived in each of the districts in question. Where they constituted the dominant ethnic group, which they did in Bushwick and Upper East Harlem, La Guardia edged over the 50 per cent mark. And where, as in the case of Lower East Harlem, they made the Eighteenth Assembly District the most densely packed Latin assembly district in greater New York, La Guardia piled up his highest score in the city: 54.02 per cent.

12 ASSEMBLY DISTRICTS

MAYORALTY ELECTION: 1933

O'Brien	McKee	Charles Solomon (Socialist)	La Guardia
%	%	%	%
45.16	6.71	1.77	45.21
31.49	11.28	2.32	54.02
29.01	16.95	2.37	50.62
18.79	33.69	2.93	42.39
21.10	21.74	5.08	47.76
35.76	15.46	3.33	43.94
29.72	16.96	7.16	44.35
34.81	19.26	1.71	43.89
28.02	17.44	2.60	50.80
19.33	19.43	4.99	53.93
23.35	22.43	3.11	49.68
20.77	23.73	7.00	44.68
28.11	18.76	3.70	47.60
27.27	28.31	2.78	40.37

To win by a majority in a multi-cornered race is something
of a feat, but Fiorello's spectacular showing in East Harlem
barely suggests the enthusiasm for him in Little Italy. Fully to
appreciate it we must sample election districts *within* assembly
districts. Whereas no assembly district in the city, not even
the Negro Twenty-first, was so "pure" as to consist of a single
ethnic group, quite a few of the almost four thousand election
districts (they averaged six hundred voters) were from 80 to
99 per cent composed of this or that nationality. Here Italian,
there Jewish, or Irish, German, Polish, Norwegian, Puerto
Rican, and so on, the sum of those ancestral enclaves made
most of the city's sixty-two assembly districts as heterogeneous as the old Austro-Hungarian Empire.

The Fifteenth Assembly District in Brooklyn's Greenpoint
was one such district, for although predominantly Irish and led
by a Last Hurrah tribal chieftain, famed Peter J. McGuinness,
it had a cosmopolitan sprinkling of Polish, German, Jewish,
and Italian colonies. Wedged between the East River and
Newtown Creek, it was the most depressed area in the wasteland stretching across the borough's waterfront from Astoria
to Red Hook. Few assembly districts were more gut Democratic than Kings County's Fifteenth. In 1932 it went to
Roosevelt by a margin of five to one, and a year later gave La
Guardia his rock bottom low in Brooklyn: 22 per cent. But in
the sole election district in all of Greenpoint that was overwhelmingly Italian, the Twenty-eighth, La Guardia crushed
O'Brien by seven votes to one and McKee by twenty to one,
receiving like Roosevelt before him a return in excess of 80 per
cent.[11]

He repeated that performance with only minor variations
throughout Brooklyn in election districts where Italo-Americans constituted 80 per cent and more of the enrolled electorate. He carried one Bushwick precinct by 317 votes to
O'Brien's 29 and McKee's 22, and another in the savage Red
Hook–Gowanus section by a score of 534 to his opponents'
combined 59. Up in Williamsburg the count was La Guardia
563, O'Brien 53, and McKee 26; down in Gravesend it was 312
for La Guardia, 18 for McKee, and 16 for O'Brien.[12] And so it
went in the other Little Italys in Brooklyn, in Brownsville and

Bensonhurst, Fort Hamilton, East New York, and Canarsie—La Guardia, in nearly every instance, taking from 80 to 89 per cent of the vote.

Over in Manhattan's Second Assembly District south of Washington Square not even the presence of the brutal Tammany boss, Al Marinelli, could prevent the Twenty-ninth Election District from casting four ballots out of five for the Little Flower. In East Harlem, where Marcantonio managed the Fusion campaign and guarded the polls, La Guardia's count rose to 386 while his two opponents' fell to a combined 45. Farther north, in the Tremont section of the Bronx, the *paesani* stampeded to their hero in majorities ranging up to 92 per cent.[13]

In Queens and Staten Island—but there is no need to go on with examples, for the dense rows of figures in the *Official Canvass of the Vote Cast* add up to a single conclusion confirmed again and again; namely, that in Latin election districts La Guardia ran ahead of his return from the city as a whole by 40 to 50 per cent of the votes. To say that there was a contest for the Italian vote would be euphemistic. McKee and O'Brien weren't the Little Flower's opponents; they were his victims. He butchered one or the other of them not by a mere two or five votes to one, but by ten and twenty and sometimes thirty votes to one!

Awesome in itself, the magnitude of that victory was all the more phenomenal because it took place only one year after the leader of La Guardia's Republican Party, Herbert Hoover, had been buried by a Latin landslide for the Democratic Roosevelt. La Guardia reversed—if one may be pardoned a questionable metaphor—the landslide. The next table measures the reversal in the most densely populated Italo-American section of the Bronx, a borough in which the Republican Party had virtually ceased to exist and Roosevelt had received his greatest margin of victory over Hoover (70.13 to 19.14 per cent).

To say that New York City was in 1933 the largest Italian (and also the largest Irish, German, and Jewish) city in the world is of course a cliché. Yet nothing could have been more profoundly significant for La Guardia than the presence of 1,070,355 New Yorkers of Italian birth or descent. Constitut-

A COMPARISON OF THE 1932 AND 1933 ELECTIONS
*Six Predominantly Italo-American Election Districts
in the Seventh Assembly District of the Bronx.*[14]

Election Districts	% for Roosevelt	% for Hoover	% for La Guardia	% for O'Brien	% for McKee
Forty-third	81.43	12.32	82.63	5.78	8.74
Forty-fourth	86.99	8.06	83.89	7.38	6.93
Forty-fifth	84.12	9.77	87.34	7.22	3.13
Forty-sixth	88.60	7.15	91.56	3.49	2.88
Forty-seventh	90.78	4.96	86.39	7.10	5.20
Forty-eighth	89.88	6.17	88.15	2.36	7.58
AVERAGE	86.98	8.07	86.66	5.55	5.74
7TH A.D. AVERAGE	72.41	12.90	47.76	21.10	21.74
BRONX AVERAGE	70.31	19.14	37.89	23.34	32.81

ing a little more than 15 per cent of the population, Italo-Americans cast at least 15 per cent of the ballots,* or some 345,000 votes, in the municipal election of 1933. That Fiorello did not get all of them is evident from the results just rendered, but Ed Corsi, head of the Italian Fusion Committee, exaggerated only slightly on Election Day night when he issued this jubilant I-told-you-so press release to the Italian-language newspapers in America.

"As we predicted," he crowed, "the more than three hundred thousand Italian votes received by the Honorable La Guardia have determined the victory of the Fusionist ticket. The new Mayor has received around ninety per cent of the entire Italian vote of New York City."[15]

Fiorello could count as well as his manager, but expressed himself more elegantly than in the language of the numbers game. According to *Il Progresso*, which advertised itself as THE FIRST AND GREATEST ITALIAN DAILY NEWSPAPER IN THE UNITED STATES, La Guardia's first words on learning the results

* That is how the experts calculate the proportion of the vote that an ethnic group casts to the total vote, and although Italian immigrants constituted half the colony's population and had a low naturalization rate, Italo-Americans voted in greater number in the 1933 election than the one in 1932.

of November 7 were these as translated from the Italian in which they were delivered:

"My first thought, my first greeting, deriving from profound gratitude, go to the Italo-American voters, who have sustained me with such cordiality, with such enthusiasm and with such faith in this memorable electoral battle.

"I should like to thank all of you, if it were possible, one by one, personally, affectionately. Your plebiscite has moved me profoundly.

"I hope to be always more worthy of your esteem and of your faithfulness."[16]

There was dancing in the streets on Election Day night from South Brooklyn to the North Bronx, and *Il Progresso* wrote that it was impossible to describe the delirium that surged through the Italian colony. For itself that journal exclaimed: "Finally the greatest city in the world has an Italian Mayor. Viva Il Nostro Fiorello La Guardia!"[17]

Long live *our* Fiorello—in that pronoun, the most collectively possessive pronoun in any language, lies the character of the Italian vote in 1933. Only a small part of it, symbolized by a Corsi or a Marcantonio or a progressive trade-union leader like August Bellanca, went to the victor because he was a liberal reformer. The major portion of it went to him because his name was then the most famous Italian name in American politics. That is why Italo-Americans, although ordinarily as Democratic in their voting behavior as their Irish and Polish and German neighbors in slums like Greenpoint, bolted their party in near unanimity for La Guardia. In 1933 they had less wealth, less prestige, less political power than any other immigrant group of comparable size in New York City. It was inevitable that they would link La Guardia's quest for success with their own desire for recognition and acceptance in the painful and awkward process of Americanization.

"The Italian-Americans have definitely decided," a Brooklyn leader of the colony wrote to Fiorello one week before the election, "and have jumped the traces of party lines and will cast a vote for you."[18]

But Italians the world over, not just those in New York

City, were stirred by the municipal election of 1933. "Italian Candidate Setback to Tammany," an Argentinian newspaper's headlines announced to the huge Italian colony. "He unites in himself the best constructive qualities of our race," boasted another newspaper in Mussolini's Rome. One of Il Duce's emissaries to the United States, the celebrated General Italo Balbo, toasted the Fusion standard-bearer during the campaign as a "magnificent co-national."[19]

To vote for anyone else but La Guardia, warned an editorial writer for the *Sons of Italy Magazine*, would be a betrayal of an ancestral obligation:

> For nearly a score of years a struggle has been carried on by those of our race in America for public recognition in the populous centers in which live substantial numbers of Italo-Americans.
>
> Self-preservation seems to be a fundamental instinct of nature, and selfishness, unfortunately, is one of the traits of the larger number of human beings. The tendency has therefore been for those of other racial origins who had preceded us in this country to retain the privileges they had taken for themselves, enlarge them, if possible, and exclude others as long as possible from a just portion of representation in the public offices. The struggle carried on by those of our blood has already netted some fruits; in some cases of relative importance, in others sporadic in nature.
>
> In helping to elevate one of our race to an important public office it must be remembered that we are helping ourselves and our individual aspirations for future realization because in almost each case the occupancy of a public office by an Italo-American establishes a precedent for that office which then receives permanent consideration. What is important, then, is to win some of these offices for the first time.[20]

Il Minatore, a weekly published for miners in the Upper Peninsula of Michigan, echoed the sentiment:

> The American citizens of Italian extraction in New York City have in their power the performance of a beautiful as well as a sacred duty. Major Fiorello H. La Guardia is one of the three candidates for the second most important elective office in America, that of mayor of New York City. If La Guardia is elected mayor of New York City the young genera-

tion of Italo-Americans will have taken a gigantic step in the assertion of their rights in American public life. Therefore, the eyes of Italo-Americans in all parts of the United States are focused on New York City for the next few days! Therefore is it the impellent duty of all the voters of Italian extraction in the five boroughs composing the largest city in the world to make their contribution to the cause and, regardless of party affiliations, of factions, of personal and of any and all other considerations, to perform what should be a pleasant duty to help in the election to that high office of a man who bears an Italian name.[21]

The enthusiasm was unprecedented because Italo-Americans believed that their kind, the most numerous of the most recent newcomers to the largest of the big cities in the United States, stood at long last on the threshold of a major breakthrough in American politics. The chief symbol of that breakthrough, La Guardia was also the beneficiary of the self-consciousness that was making it possible. For the first time in a New York City election, Generoso Pope's *Il Progresso* exulted, fourteen candidates were of Italian descent. Although a Tammany pitchman for years, Pope publicized all fourteen irrespective of party, issues, or merit.[22] On election night the colony celebrated not only the triumph of that "magnificent co-national" La Guardia but also the victory of that worthy gentleman from the Second Assembly District, Boss Al Marinelli, who was elected county clerk.

No one understood better than the Little Flower himself that what the newspapers of the day called "pride of race" lay behind the *Risorgimento* of 1933. He nursed that pride, soothed that pride, inflated that pride, manipulated that pride, all the while taking care that that pride should not be injured. He might appeal to the Jews by lashing out against Hitler, but as for Mussolini, whom he privately loathed but who together with himself was the chief political source of Latin pride in the city, Fiorello observed, as he had in the past, a policy of public silence. More, he labored behind the scenes to get anti-Fascists and Fascists in the colony to ignore their differences and concentrate on the municipal election.

It was in that spirit that his managers persuaded Generoso Pope, a great admirer of Mussolini, to report the campaign without taking sides on the issues or the parties involved (*Viva il nostro La Guardia!* and *Viva il nostro Marinelli!*). And when another newspaperman, the editor of *Il Lazio*, saluted Mussolini and La Guardia as the two greatest living Italians in the world, Fiorello didn't burst into a fit of temper and sue for libel, but instead invited the man to have a talk with Ed Corsi, "who I am sure," he wrote gently, "will be very much interested in your work." Corsi abominated Fascism as much as did La Guardia, but the strategy of 1933 called for transcending, not igniting, the most explosive issue in the colony.[23]

If that was Fiorello's aim, his tactic was to build a consensus around his own person and personality. In a characteristic speech before a mass meeting held under the auspices of the Italian Division of the General Fusion Committee at the Hippodrome Theater on Sixth Avenue and West Forty-third Street, the son of Achille Luigi Carlo La Guardia said: "Our opponents can defame my name and disparage my career but cannot deprive me of your affection." That was the kind of talk to unify the colony—"*our* opponents . . . *my* name . . . *your* affection"—for that was the kind of talk the colony wanted to hear. Even before the balloting began *Il Progresso* declaimed:

—*Viva il nostro Fiorello!*
—*Viva La Guardia!*
—*Viva il nuovo Sindaco [new Mayor] di New York!*[24]

3. *The Jewish Vote: A Study in Volatility*

It has often been said that La Guardia was as popular with the Jewish voters of New York City as the Roosevelt and Lehman they idolized. But not even during the height of his considerable appeal to such voters in 1937 and 1941 did the Mayor receive Jewish majorities as fabulous as those bestowed on the President and the governor. As for the election of 1933, the most volatile vote of all that year was the Jewish vote. La Guardia won a larger share of it than did McKee or O'Brien, but the results by district varied so extremely that the Mayor-elect ran brilliantly in some Jewish precincts while losing badly in others.

It has also been said, and this point has been made by nearly every writer on the subject, that La Guardia won the election of 1933 because he knocked McKee out of the race on the charge of anti-Semitism. The interpretation sounds plausible, for it rests on the premise that the alienation of 1,825,000 Jews, who constituted a little more than a fourth of the electorate, must surely have led to defeat. Yet no one has offered reliable evidence that the Jews as a body were leaning toward McKee before La Guardia accused him of being a bigot and that they then abandoned him in large numbers.[25]

Without that kind of information it is impossible to say precisely how many votes McKee lost to La Guardia, or for that matter, to O'Brien. The election results are of little help in measuring such losses and gains; for the three candidates, and the Socialist Charles Solomon as well, received Jewish returns on average either equal to their respective city-wide scores or not sufficiently different to affect the outcome of the contest. The Jews as a whole voted, in short, like New York City as a whole. In so doing they not only expressed their own very acute internal differences but also symbolized the kaleidoscopic character of one of the more mixed-up elections in the twentieth century.

None of this is meant to suggest that McKee was not staggered and even hurt by the burden that LaGuardia strapped to his sensitive and vulnerable back. Although defeating his tormentor in some Jewish election districts, the Bronx Democrat lost his home borough, the most Democratic and the most Jewish in the city, and failed indeed to carry a single predominantly Jewish assembly district there or anywhere else in New York. Yet one wonders how much La Guardia hurt himself because of the part he played in the climactic episode of the campaign. Not only did he antagonize the ultras among the anti-Semites, but as the influential *American Hebrew* put it scorchingly:

"The Jews of New York have nothing to be grateful for to those responsible for the intrusion of the Jewish issue in the present political situation. We are not advocating the election of any of the candidates for Mayor of New York," that journal continued its criticism of La Guardia, "but we protest against the type of politics and the character of politicians

who, after our national experience of 1928, wll resurrect and
acclaim a religious issue for the sake of vote-getting."[26]

The first step toward understanding the Jewish response to
La Guardia in 1933 requires that one put aside any notion that
it was homogeneous. Heterogeneity is the key to the Jewish
volatility of 1933. Unlike the Italians, who were largely prole-
tarian, overwhelmingly Democratic, and united by a demand
for political recognition they believed long overdue, the Jews
belonged to all income groups, lived in every grade of neighborhood from the squalid Lower East Side to comfortable
Borough Park to swank Riverside Drive, voted in significant
numbers for Socialists and Republicans if most often for
Democrats, and achieved political recognition a good many
years before the election of Governor Herbert Lehman in
1932. It was almost symbolic of their headstart over the
Italians that the first New York Italo-American politician of
consequence, La Guardia, should have been half Jewish.

That part of his ancestry was unknown at the time except to
a few intimate friends, so that Jews shared none of the Italo-
American frenzy to mass behind the Little Flower for ancestral reasons. What is more, unlike the mere fourteen Italo-
American candidates, so many Jews ran for office in 1933 that
the *American Hebrew* reminded its readers that they ought to
be beyond ethnic bloc voting. And whereas Generoso Pope's
three newspapers gave a blanket endorsement to all and only
Latin office-seekers, the Yiddish-language press divided, char-
acteristically, along traditional party lines.

The sole newspaper in that language for Fiorello was the
Morning Journal, a Republican organ that had opposed Roosevelt in 1932 with the dire warning that his election would be as
catastrophic as Woodrow Wilson's in 1912 and Grover Cleveland's in 1892. The *Day* had long been associated with Tammany Hall and came out as a matter of course for John Patrick
O'Brien, while the Communist *Freiheit* backed a party slate
headed by a non-Jewish Texan by the name of Robert Minor.
As for the celebrated *Forward*, which would be in La Guardia's camp by 1937, it attacked La Guardia as the machine
candidate of a reactionary party and endorsed, as it had for
more than thirty years, the Socialist ticket.[27]

But the distribution of 554,000 Jewish ballots was far more important for the outcome of the mayoral contest than editorial opinion in the immigrant press, and we must therefore turn once again to a comparison of the election of 1933 with that of 1932.*

The results for the Presidency from the eighteen most heavily concentrated Jewish assembly districts averaged out to 70 per cent Democratic, 19 per cent Republican, 9 per cent Socialist, and the remainder Communist and Socialist Labor. A random sample of a hundred election districts confirms the Democratic proportion but raises the Socialist and lowers the Republican by a few percentage points. It is therefore not far from the mark to say that Roosevelt received, in round numbers, 387,000 Jewish votes, Hoover from 95,000 to 105,000, and Norman Thomas between 50,000 and 60,000 (the latter was, incidentally, about half Thomas's 122,565 total from all voters).

In the same districts, as the table on the next page shows in detail, La Guardia averaged 42 per cent, while McKee and O'Brien vied neck and neck at respectively 26 and 25 per cent, and Solomon dropped to half Thomas's percentage. Like Republican support in general, the Jewish Republican vote held up for Fusion. But Socialist and Democratic erosions took place, and of the two the Democratic shift toward La Guardia was the most important in numbers. The combined McKee-O'Brien Jewish tally of 283,000 fell below Roosevelt's by just over 100,000 ballots.

Like the Italians, then, a sizable bloc of Jewish Democrats came over to the Fusionist Fiorello. But more of them remained loyal to their party through both McKee and O'Brien, who together outscored La Guardia better than two to one among Jewish Democrats, whereas the Little Flower swept the colony, as we have seen, by staggering majorities. What is equally important, the Jewish Democrats for La Guardia generally belonged to higher economic levels than the Italians

---

*Since only a negligible one per cent fewer New Yorkers voted in 1933 than in 1932, we can assume that in both years the Jews cast about 550,000 ballots, in proportion to their 27 per cent of the electorate.

and in overwhelming numbers began disengaging themselves from the local Democracy before the Fusion movement of 1933.

Their defection got under way in the special 1932 mayoral campaign when they gave the Russian-born Morris Hillquit a major portion of his 249,887 total. Unequaled by either Eugene Debs or Norman Thomas, that figure still stands as a record for a Socialist candidate in New York City. But although the national chairman of his party and one of its leading theoreticians since he had helped to found it at the turn of the century, Hillquit was a conservative and personally magnetic Marxist who appealed to non-Socialists.[29] That is largely why he ran 60,000 votes ahead of his party's choice for President and governor (Louis Waldman) combined.

Like the write-in sentiment for McKee, the expression for Hillquit in 1932 was in good part a protest vote against O'Brien and the impossible Tammany bosses behind him. The Socialist did particularly well in Jewish precincts that Roosevelt and Lehman swept by from twenty-five to thirty-five percentage points above O'Brien's score. Anti-Tammany in local politics but a mixture of New Deal Democrat and Socialist (Hillquit's share of Thomas's return) in national affairs, the Hillquit vote was a hybrid vote. The turnout for him, which a year later went substantially to La Guardia, apart from a hardcore Marxian 59,846 to the unappealing Solomon, was a pre-

THE JEWISH VOTE

Borough	Jewish Votes by Borough	Proportion of Jewish Votes to Borough Votes	La Guardia			McKee		
			Jewish Votes	Jewish %	Borough-Wide %	Jewish Votes	Jewish %	Borough-Wide %
Manhattan	85,683	16%	32,388	37.80	37.99	19,896	23.22	23.09
Brooklyn	252,742	33.3%	111,055	43.94	43.72	60,254	23.84	25.63
Bronx	184,046	46%	72,441	39.36	37.89	55,048	29.91	32.81
Queens	31,530°	8%	15,084	47.84	39.16	7,744	24.56	35.85
City	554,001	27%	230,968	41.69	40.37	142,942	25.80	28.31

° No assembly district in Queens was predominantly Jewish. The figures for that 0.2 per cent of the city's Jews lived in that borough, and the negligible 1,200 votes the Jewish population by borough, see C. Morris Horowitz, Lawrence J. Kaplan,

view of the political realignment that was to take place a few years later in the creation of New York's American Labor Party.

Loyal Republicans, Hillquit-Thomas Socialists, plus Roosevelt-Lehman Democrats continuing their defection of 1932—that was how the Jewish vote distributed itself for La Guardia. But the proportions varied from one area of the city to another, reflecting the diversity of the Jewish community. Who among the Jews, then, furnished La Guardia an estimated 231,000 votes? The answer to that question lies in an examination of districts according to nativity, income, education, and political affiliation.

A little more than 100,000 of Manhattan's estimated 297,000 Jews lived south of East Fourteenth Street. The remnants of a colony once five times that size, they were the least successful, the least assimilated, and therefore the least mobile of their ethnic group. The same was true of their non-Jewish neighbors of almost every extraction. Popularly called the Lower East Side, the area between Fourteenth Street and the Manhattan Bridge had a higher density of population per square mile, a larger proportion of foreign-born to natives, and a lower median annual family expenditure ($1,358) than any area of comparable size in Greater New York.[30]

Bisected by Delancey Street and containing the famous

18 ASSEMBLY DISTRICTS[28]

O'Brien			Solomon			Others		
Jewish Votes	Jewish %	Borough-Wide %	Jewish Votes	Jewish %	Borough-Wide %	Jewish Votes	Jewish %	Borough-Wide %
29,492	34.42	35.97	2,442	2.85	1.96	1,465	1.71	.09
61,644	24.39	25.60	13,041	5.16	3.54	6,748	2.67	2.38
42,735	23.22	23.34	8,153	4.43	3.68	5,669	3.08	2.28
6,921	21.95	22.96	1,378	4.37	1.69	404	1.28	.34
140,792	25.49	27.27	25,014	4.52	2.78	14,286	2.58	1.27

borough are based on election districts in the Rockaways. As for Staten Island, only or so that they cast need not be included in the calculation. For the distribution of *The Jewish Population of the New York Area, 1900–1975* (New York, 1959), 94, 96.

Orchard Street Pushcart Market, the Fourth Assembly District lay in the heart of the Jewish quarter. In 1932 awarding both Governor Lehman and President Roosevelt their highest highs in the city, respectively 90 and 91 per cent, the Fourth also gave the Socialist Hillquit one of his lower lows. La Guardia's return a year later? Twenty-three per cent. It would have been less had not a minority of Italo-American voters broken in the usual numbers for Fiorello, for his Jewish losses were so severe in the Fourth that in one election district where almost none but Jews lived—the Twenty-fourth on Broome, Essex, Delancey, Ludlow, and Rivington Streets—La Guardia was defeated by O'Brien 73.86 to 9.65 per cent. The year before Lehman carried the same precinct by an unbelievable majority of 99.45 per cent, and Roosevelt by an only slightly less fantastic 99.17 per cent!

Next door, however, in the less but still predominantly Jewish Sixth Assembly District, the veteran Republican boss, Sam Koenig, rallied what remained of the party faithful behind the G.O.P. standard-bearer. Not enough to overcome O'Brien's winning 46.48 per cent, La Guardia's 36.42 return in the Sixth was at least a good deal more respectable than his dismal showing in the rock-ribbed Democratic Fourth (whose leader, incidentally, was an Irishman, Eddie Ahearn). But in the other adjacent district, the Eighth, a small swing vote of Hillquit Socialists joined a larger bloc of Italian Democrats and Republicans of all ethnic origins to edge La Guardia just past O'Brien.

Taken as a whole, La Guardia's average on the Lower East Side was 33.21 per cent to O'Brien's 40.83 per cent, McKee's 19.24 per cent, and Solomon's measly 3.86 per cent.

Those results were roughly duplicated in the other ten Manhattan assembly districts that fell to O'Brien. None was significantly Jewish. But like those on the Lower East Side, they were gut Democratic and with only two exceptions, Manhattanville and lower Washington Heights, lay in blighted or partly blighted sections: in the Gashouse District, Yorkville and Spanish Harlem, Battery Park, the lower West Side, and Hell's Kitchen. Clearly, like the poorest of the Irish and Germans, the poorest of the Czechs, Poles, and Puerto Ricans, the poorest of the poor Jews in Manhattan voted in greatest number for Tammany.

It is understandable that McKee should have been ground to pieces by the Manhattan machine as a traitor, and nowhere was the mutilation more horrible than in the toughest Irish wards along the Hudson River. But how is one to account for what happened to La Guardia? There he was, touted as a man of the people and a champion of the foreign-born and the poor, yet losing polyglot slums (unless they were inhabited by Italo-Americans) while sweeping Park Avenue precincts by actual majorities. In fact, with only three middle-class exceptions, the only assembly districts to reject La Guardia corresponded to areas that the Department of Health daintily called Sore Spots.

Merely to describe what occurred is really to explain it, for in the history of American municipal politics the stiffest resistance to antimachine movements has come from the river wards, the waterfront precincts, the districts of the disinherited. To La Guardia and the sternly moralistic Seabury the boss was an enemy of the people and the system by which he ruled therefore had to be destroyed. But to the very poor, irrespective of ethnic background, the boss was not a menace but a benefactor. He was the man to see when you needed a job, or a liquor or a pushcart license, when you were in trouble with the police or even with your wife. In return he asked only for your vote. And if he filled his own pocket, that was acceptable in a hard world where everyone was expected to look out for himself and his own. La Guardia and Seabury were, in short, most against what the poor were most for: government by favor and connections. It was the only kind of local government they had known and could therefore understand.

Conversely, the native American middle and upper classes historically have provided the leadership, and in large measure the electorate, for municipal reform movements. To such citizens the best government is impartial, dispensing favors to none and dedicated to the efficient and economical promotion of the generalized public good. As for public office, it is a trust, not a form of private property, an obligation—better, a calling—to selfless service. In Samuel Seabury, the Mayflower descendant and namesake of the first Episcopal bishop in the United States, and John Curry, the Irish-born but lower West Side–bred heir to the machine Boss Tweed constructed, we have the epitome of the collision in values that occurred in New York City in 1933.[31]

Call this cluster of ideas just discussed what you will—the Protestant Ethic, the American Creed, Political Puritanism, or Issue Politics—a significant number of middle-class and well-to-do Jews believed in them. And so the Jewish vote broke for La Guardia along class lines. Thus he carried the Central Park West Seventh and Ninth Assembly Districts, where the wealthiest Jews of the city lived, by 20 percentage points above his return from the Lower East Side Fourth, receiving in some election districts as much as 58 per cent of the vote.[32]

The nine votes to one against La Guardia on Delancey Street and the close to three votes out of five for him in the West Seventies expressed the will of polar opposites in the Jewish community. No other assembly district was comparable to Central Park West's in the numbers of educated, upper middle-class, assimilated Jews divided almost equally between Democrats and Republicans, and none was as poor, foreign-born, Yiddish-speaking, and subservient to Tammany Hall as the Lower East Side's Fourth. What is more, Manhattan contained only 16 per cent of the city's Jewish population. Almost half the Jews made Brooklyn their home, and a third the Bronx. The majority in both boroughs lived neither below the poverty line nor on the gold coast but somewhere in between.

What was that somewhere in between?

In *New York City Market Analysis*, a book containing data from the 1930 census for the use of merchants, the city was divided into districts according to annual family expenditure. The areas of middle-class settlement, colored orange on the maps, housed families in the $3,000 to $4,999 a year bracket.* Those of higher status lived in districts colored red, purple or gold, those of lower status in districts colored green or blue. The more one went up the scale, moreover, the larger the proportion one found of assimilated and educated persons. If

---

* To arrive at comparable figures for the same class today, one would have to more than double those reported in the 1930 census.

we may render La Guardia's Jewish return in market colors, he lost the blue vote of less than $1,800 a year, but scored well above his city-wide 40 per cent beginning in orange precincts, and averaged around 35 per cent or so of the green ballots in the roughly $2,500-a-year class.

The influence of the last-named class is best seen in the Bronx, which housed a predominantly lower-income Jewish community constituting 46 per cent of that borough's entire population. Only one assembly district, Tremont's Seventh, with a large Latin vote, returned La Guardia enthusiastically: 47.76 per cent. More typical of his reception in the Bronx was the behavior of Morrisania's Fifth. One of the densest Jewish quarters in the city and having a median annual family expediture of $2,770, it went to La Guardia—but fourteen points below his Tremont high.

The point about Morrisania, and other green areas like it, is that it was not only strongly Democratic but more Socialist and Communist than districts *both* poorer *and* wealthier. Therein lies the reason for La Guardia's winning but mediocre 34 per cent; Charles Solomon and Robert Minor together took a little more than 10 per cent of the vote in the Fifth. In the solid middle-income belt along the Grand Concourse of the west Bronx's Second Assembly District, on the other hand, Fiorello broke loose and ran in the forties.[33] His Bronx return as a whole, 37.89 per cent, was his lowest in the five boroughs.

Queens may serve as an almost pure example of the voting behavior of Jews above the $3,000-a-year line. Too small in numbers to make any of the six assembly districts predominantly Jewish, most of the 88,000 Jews of the borough lived in such scattered middle-class communities as Jackson Heights, Forest Hills, South Jamaica, and the Rockaways. Roosevelt-Lehman Democrats and Hillquit Socialists, the sort who had voted a split ticket in 1932, they were the stuff Fusion fans were made of. Comfortable Rockaway neighborhoods went over to Fiorello, for example, in the high forty percentages.[34]

But it was Brooklyn, the home of 851,000 Jews, that exemplified the behavior of New York City's Jewish electorate as a whole in 1933. Its class structure was less uniform than Queens' but more so than Manhattan's and included a larger proportion than the Bronx's of both the very poor and the solid middle-class and home-owning element. A paradigm of the city's Jewish population, Brooklyn stands as a microcosm of the blue, green, and orange votes where neither McKee nor O'Brien ran as the native son and the local (McCooey) machine had broken down under the weight of feuding Flynn and Curry stalwarts.

Roughly 15 per cent of the Jewish families lived on or below the poverty line of $1,800 a year, and the best illustration of how they voted is Williamsburg's Fourteenth Assembly District which was around half Jewish, two-fifths Italian, and the remainder Polish and Irish. Two of the predominantly Jewish precincts went to McKee, four declared for La Guardia, and eight swung to O'Brien. The overwhelming favorite of the Irish and the Poles was McKee, and it is almost unnecessary to add that the Italian election districts formed the usual solid phalanxes behind the Little Flower. And so, in spite of losing two Jewish precincts in three to O'Brien, La Guardia carried predominantly Jewish Williamsburg by a 39 per cent plurality.[35]

In Brownsville's Twenty-third Assembly District, whose voting behavior was typical of the 35 per cent or so of Brooklyn's Jewish families with annual expenditures of around $2,500, La Guardia triumphed by a handsome 45 per cent and carried all but a few precincts. But Solomon and Minor ran ahead of themselves in that Marxian stronghold, with the result that La Guardia's returns from Jewish election districts ranged from the twenties into the thirties and only rarely beyond. How, then, was he able in the Twenty-third Assembly District to surpass his city-wide plurality of 40 per cent? The answer by now should be obvious. The way was cleared for the Little Flower by a Latin landslide.[36]

And then the Jewish vote broke to La Guardia in unmistakable accents. In Crown Heights and East Flatbush, Manhattan Beach and Seagate, Midwood and Borough Park, Bensonhurst, Flatlands and Sheepshead Bay, there was none of Williamsburg's blind vote for the machine and little of Brownsville's meager assents grudgingly given, but unequivocal mandates in the forties, in the fifties, and on occasion in the sixties.[37] This was La Guardia country, extending from Eastern

Parkway to Coney Island, and settled since World War I by a new middle class of first- and second-generation Americans. On the market analysis maps the area was a huge orange swath, with splashes of red and purple and an occasional flash of gold.

La Guardia's most ardent support came from Roosevelt-Lehman precincts so anti-Tammany that in 1932 they not only denied O'Brien a majority but in several instances defeated him by going for Hillquit. But middle-class Brooklyn was only partly Jewish, and in two of the three assembly districts below Eastern Parkway, the Second and the Eighteenth, Irish and German and other voters held down La Guardia's plurality to 44 per cent. However, in the Sixteenth Assembly District, where a substantial number of lower-income Italians neutralized La Guardia's losses, he triumphed by a score roughly equal to his average in Jewish election districts: 53.93 per cent.[38]

His high in Brooklyn, it yielded first place in the city only to the 54.02 per cent returned by the Eighteenth Assembly District in La Guardia's own East Harlem.

Brooklyn's Jewish population divided about equally into families above the $3,000-a-year living and those below it.[39] If one averages the election results from both groups, La Guardia's return comes out to 43.94 per cent. It was a fraction higher than his borough-wide score, while McKee's and O'Brien's were each a point lower. As Kings County went so went the Jews who lived there. They stood on dead center between the fantastic highs for Fiorello in Little Italy and his abysmal lows among the poorest and therefore most gut Democratic Irish, Germans, and Poles.

4. *Pro-Italianism, Not Anti-Semitism*

"The damage had been done by the assertion that McKee was anti-Semitic," Ed Flynn has written in his memoirs. "McKee's repeated attempts to show that his entire life was a story of tolerance were of no avail." Henry Moskowitz, a La Guardia supporter and former adviser to Al Smith, put it this way in an interview in 1934: "The Jewish controversy had a great deal to do with McKee's defeat. The Jews at that time

were under the influence of the Hitler business and a great
deal of harm was done to McKee because of the anti-Semitic
articles."[40]

One could multiply endlessly the quotations to the effect
that anti-Semitism was the decisive issue of the campaign of
1933. None of these assertions has ever been accompanied by
proof. Before one can believe that McKee lost and La Guardia
won the election because of the Jewish issue, one would have
to have evidence that the Recovery candidate appealed to a
large number of Jewish voters before the explosion caused by
the republication of his Catholic views on "a most serious
problem." There is no such evidence.

McKee ran well in Jewish districts when he was elected
president of the Board of Aldermen in 1925 and re-elected in
1929. But all Democrats were returned by all Democratic
districts in those years. The times changed, and when McKee
won a phenomenal 234,000 write-in vote in the special mayoral
election of 1932, the Jews showed slight enthusiasm for his
candidacy and gave a much larger proportion of their votes
not only to Hillquit but to the Republican Lewis Pounds
as well. Ranging from a low 0.25 per cent in the Lower
East Side Fourth Assembly District to a high 14.03 per
cent in the West Bronx Second Assembly District, McKee's
average in eighteen of the city's most Jewish assembly districts
came out to 11.35 per cent. That was also his mean tally
throughout New York, among non-Jews and Jews alike.

But since in 1933 McKee more than doubled his Jewish
return of the previous year, one might argue that a trend had
developed for him and would have carried him to victory had
not La Guardia's accusation of anti-Semitism halted and di-
verted it. There is no evidence that such a trend was in the
making, and even Ed Flynn has admitted that the McKee
campaign was limping before the *Catholic World* article made
headlines. More important, as in 1932, the Jews in 1933 as a
whole voted for and against McKee in the same proportion as
did the New York City electorate as a whole. Far from being
aberrant, therefore, the Jews were a bellwether of the election of 1933.

McKee did, of course, lose votes because of his reputation for alleged anti-Semitism. If he claimed to be a friend of the Jews, Untermyer could ask, who needed enemies? But since O'Brien, who had a reputation for tolerance, did no better with the Jews than McKee and actually ran behind him in Morrisania, Brownsville, and the Rockaways, there must be other reasons in addition to anti-Semitism to explain why McKee won only a fourth of the Jewish vote.

For one thing, he and O'Brien killed each other off, dividing a Democratic vote large enough to elect one man but not two. For another, each man was burdened by the backing of a local Democratic machine. The Jewish revolt begun in 1932 and expressed through Hillquit continued into the next year to La Guardia's benefit. Here we touch the heart of the matter. The revolt in 1932 and the following year involved roughly 140,000 Jews, and La Guardia was further assured of a hard-core Republican vote of around 90,000 that had gone to Lewis Pounds in the 1932 mayoral contest. The big question, therefore, is whether McKee was the sort to appeal to the defectors.

He was not. Many of those defectors, it will be remembered, had voted for Morris Hillquit *and* Norman Thomas. Neither a social nor an economic progressive, but something of an accomplished Red-baiter, McKee could not have pleased the men and women of the Marxist gospel even had he been a founder in his youth of the Anti-Defamation League instead of a writer for the *Catholic World*. As for the Hillquit-Roosevelt-Lehman voters, they had cause to doubt that McKee was their man. Neither Roosevelt nor Lehman endorsed him, and throughout the campaign Professor Berle insisted often, in many places, and with the authority of a brain truster, that the New Deal President did not stand behind the Recovery standard bearer.

But let us for the moment agree to give all of the 140,000 or so of La Guardia's Democratic-Socialist votes to McKee. The result? Those votes would not have closed the 260,000 gap between him and La Guardia. To beat La Guardia, McKee would have needed in addition nearly all of the 141,000 Jewish votes for O'Brien. But this presupposes that most of the Jews who voted for O'Brien did so merely because they thought

McKee anti-Semitic. There is no more reason to believe that than to say that the bulk of La Guardia's Jewish support derived from the resurrection of McKee's ideas about Jewish students.

For the fact is, the Jews didn't dislike McKee *that* much. It was not they who punished the Bronx Democrat with the 10, 9, 8, 7, 6, or 5 per cent returns he received from one end of the city to the other. Those lows came from only one ethnic group, the Italians, as they piled up majorities for the Little Flower in the eighties and nineties. The most explosive ethnic issue of the campaign, and the one with the greatest significance for the outcome on Election Day, was not anti-Semitism. It was pro-Italianism.

VI

The Meaning of
the Mandate:
"The Brains of Tammany Hall
Lie in Calvary Cemetery"

La Guardia entered City Hall at the head of a coalition comprising disparate elements. Yet there could be no mistaking what was essential in his mandate. If New York City was still a Democratic town in 1933, it was even more an anti-Tammany town. The vote for O'Brien and McKee may have been 327,000 more than for La Guardia, but that for La Guardia and McKee was 891,000 more than for O'Brien. Even in Manhattan, where the Curry incumbent ran strongest, six voters in ten decided that it was time for a change. New York City had given La Guardia a mandate to clean the Wigwamean Stables.

It came from voters of every sort and condition, but in largest proportion from the middle and wealthy classes. This fits what scholars have recently discovered and professional politicians have known for a long time—that both suburbs and silk-stocking districts generate the most power for anti-boss

movements. That's how it was in 1933. Central Park East gave
La Guardia and McKee their highest joint assembly district return, and Queens furnished the two men their highest borough
return.

The most suburban part of New York City, with the largest
proportion of homeowners and native Americans, Queens
housed the kind of voters who, uncontrolled by bosses and
concerned with such problems as the tax rate and local im-
provements, responded in loudest voice (74.96 per cent) to the
La Guardia–McKee call that government by boodle and crony
must go.

And just as Central Park East was the most Protestant assembly district in New York City, Queens was the most Protestant
borough.[1] Not that all Protestants are or have been advocates of
good government—witness the Huey Long movement—but the
political expression of the Protestant Ethic has always emphasized the application of private standards of rectitude to public
affairs. Most of the men in La Guardia's inner circle, Berle and
Burlingham, Seabury and Windels, Chadbourne and Blanshard,
Tuttle and Macy, Morris and Howard, were Protestants. Nor
was it a coincidence that the La Guardia administration would
have more Protestant appointees than any administration since
that of the Brahmin Mayor Seth Low.

But the La Guardia administration would also include a
large number of Jews, and that was not due to a mere political
payoff. Davidson and Price, who at first opposed La Guardia
but ultimately supported him, spoke for a significant segment
of New Yorkers devoted to municipal reform. The Jewish
middle classes were, and had been since the 1910's, partners
with their Protestant counterparts in keeping the Protestant
Ethic alive in New York City. That more of them did so
proportionately than Catholics may have been due to the fact
that proportionately more Jews than Catholics had risen out
of the immigrant proletariat to the great American middle
class. The Protestant Ethic is, after all, synonymous with the
American Creed and Middle Class Morality.[2]

But La Guardia had also asked for a mandate to build a local
welfare state in the interests of the non-middle classes. Did he
receive it? The voters who should have responded most posi-

tively to him in this connection voted instead for McKee in Greenpoint and the South Bronx and for O'Brien in Hell's Kitchen, the Lower East Side, and other slums rimming the city. In fact, to see at a glance where La Guardia's main opposition came from, turn the pages of *New York City Market Analysis* to the maps of the blue-colored districts whose residents lived below the poverty line. The chief exception was, of course, the Italians, most of whom were poor and many very, very poor. But apart from a few intellectuals and a minority belonging to the middle classes or the progressive trade unions of the garment industry, the Italo-Americans rallied to La Guardia because, like the Fascist Mussolini, he was a famous brother who made one proud to be Latin. Recognition, not reform, was their motive.

There was no questioning the mandate, though, from the sixty thousand or so Norman Thomas Socialists who voted for La Guardia instead of Solomon and the larger number of Hillquit Socialists who declared for him. Although heavily Jewish, the Socialist ranks included New Yorkers of nearly every background. Not only that, the more doctrinaire Socialists like Abraham Cahan of the *Forward* denounced La Guardia as a servant of "the rich and the landlords," whereas the *Nation*, published by William Lloyd Garrison's grandson, backed La Guardia in the belief that he would turn New York City into a gigantic laboratory in social experimentation. "It may be that a certain percentage of my *Nation* following will be less likely to go Socialist if they know I am actively at work for you," Oswald Garrison Villard wrote to La Guardia.[3] The size of the left-of-center intellectual vote is unknown, but there can be little doubt that La Guardia got most of it.

But in terms of numbers, the La Guardia era began with less electoral support for promoting social justice than for throwing the rascals out of office. To that extent the 1933 Fusion movement was like those of 1913 and 1901: a crusade for what has been called good, not welfare, government. La Guardia therefore occupies a place in the Goo Goo tradition. But as a plain man from the plain people, Fiorello had only one thing in common with the likes of Seth Low: Protestantism.

Besides, he had talked enough about the need for social justice in the campaign to suggest the direction of his adminis-

tration. It was to move to the left as the Depression deepened
and the New Deal philosophy of government with a heart
became the official philosophy of the 1930's. The times were to
demand the social and economic liberalism La Guardia had
been preaching for years. When he ran for re-election in 1937
he would again do so as a Republican, but also and more
importantly with an endorsement from the newly founded
American Labor Party. Created by both New Deal Democrats
and New York Socialists, that party would enlarge the limited
mandate for social reconstruction that La Guardia had received in 1933.

To the extent that La Guardia received the support of
Democrats, Socialists, and Independents, he was elected mayor
in spite of being a Repubican. Therein lies the City Fusion
Party's major contribution to the outcome of 1933. It made it
possible for many people to vote for La Guardia without
having to vote Republican. The widespread and longstanding
dislike of New Yorkers for the Grand Old Party cannot be
emphasized too much, for in the forty years since President
Calvin Coolidge's election in 1924 Senator Jacob Javits has
been the only Republican to carry the city in the Republican
column alone.

But La Guardia, while overcoming the unpopularity of the
G.O.P. label, also capitalized on his affiliation with it. Contra-
dictory as the statement sounds, the mathematics of 1933 were
such that he would have gone down to defeat had not some
450,000 Republican voters remained loyal to their party's
choice. In contrast to purists who court only one kind of voter
on the theory that electoral politics is either a matter of blind
political fealty or an exercise in applied ideology, La Guardia
was a pluralist and a pragmatist who practiced the politics of
coalition. The mechanics of his coalition are relevant to any
Republican who hopes to duplicate Fiorello's feat in New York
City: a firm base in his own party, an endorsement from a
third party, defections from all other parties, and a divided
Democratic Party.

Tammany itself paved the way for La Guardia's chance to
remake New York City. And here one must say that, while it
is a mistake to underestimate the shrewdness of the old-line big-
city professional politicians, it is also an error to make them

brainier than they were. More concretely, La Guardia's debt
to Tammany's stupidity was as enormous as that stupidity was
monumental. Tammany was asinine, to leave aside the question
of ethics, to swill at the public trough in so outrageous a
manner as to invite the Seabury investigations. That was the
beginning of the Hall's downfall. What completed it was the
further absurdity of naming O'Brien as La Guardia's rival. Not
only was the incumbent a preposterous figure in 1933, but his
renomination resulted in the Roosevelt-Flynn-Farley conclave
to run McKee. That intervention split the Democratic vote
and, although it may not have been the President's intention,
terminated in La Guardia's victory.

"The division in the party," Boss McCooey of Brooklyn
complained bitterly, "cost us the election." Jim Farley said
much the same though in a different spirit: "We lose but
Tammany doesn't win." And this is how La Guardia put it
shortly after the election in a speech before the Legislative
Correspondents' Dinner in Albany: "Before I do anything or
say anything here tonight, I want to thank one man who, more
than any other man, is responsible for my election as Mayor—
Jim Farley. Put it there, Jim." Farley flushed, then shook La
Guardia's hand, while the room burst into laughter.[4]

The question has often been asked if La Guardia would have
defeated O'Brien by a majority if McKee had not entered the
race and taken anti-Tammany votes from La Guardia. The
answer is probably yes. The *Literary Digest*, which successfully predicted the outcome of the contest in successive polls
from September up to Election Day, had La Guardia way
ahead of O'Brien before it became a three-way campaign.
Roosevelt intervened, moreover, after the results of both the
polls and the September primaries pointed toward the Democrats' losing the city to Fusion. But in the end none of this is
conclusive, and it is doubtful if we shall ever be sure of what
would have happened.

Nor can we be certain of the answer to a question still more
intriguing but less often asked, namely, would La Guardia
have beaten McKee had McKee been the incumbent in a two-
cornered race? The question isn't altogether fanciful, for
Flynn had sought McKee's nomination in both 1932 and 1933.
By every rule of common sense he deserved it. The first

concern of professional politics is to survive through a winning candidate, and McKee had proved a good vote-getter both as a state legislator and as president of the Board of Alderman. Moreover, a political leader is supposed to please a variety of people, and McKee had done that as acting mayor. There was, finally, no reason to question his party loyalty in 1932 or before September of 1933, for he had said publicly that he was proud to be an organization Democrat. One can only suppose that Curry's choice of O'Brien over McKee manifested an oddly political form of the death wish.

Now, if O'Brien, an affable incompetent, could have been elected in 1932—with the stink of the Seabury investigations still burning in New York's nose—is it not possible that McKee would have done the same that year? And is it not even more within the realm of possibility that he would have given a less ludicrous performance as mayor and, therefore, have been a harder man for La Guardia to beat? Above all and beyond everything else, McKee would have been a formidable opponent, as La Guardia knew, if he had not had to share the party vote with another Democrat. There is, of course, no telling how many of his anti-machine votes McKee, as a Tammany incumbent, would have lost to La Guardia, but it is still hard not to believe that 1933 *could* have been a horse race if Curry had shown more horse sense.

It is even harder to imagine Curry's comedy of errors being produced when Charles F. Murphy headed the Hall. The Gashouse boy had scrubbed the Tiger's face after the dirty Croker regime and, although he made mistakes, he judged men and events with extraordinary shrewdness. During the Progressive Era, when New Yorkers wanted reform, Murphy sponsored such outstanding Democrats as Al Smith and Robert F. Wagner, Sr. Even La Guardia admired Murphy for his understanding of what people wanted. Curry was an intellectual pygmy by comparison. Unimaginative, stubborn, rigid, and senseless, he ran the organization Seabury investigated. Jimmy Walker pronounced the epitaph for the local Democracy when he said, of Murphy's death in 1924: "The brains of Tammany Hall lie in Calvary Cemetery."[5]

Much has been written about politics in terms of aspirations, but not enough has been said of the politics of resentment. We would miss the significance of 1933 if we failed to understand that resentment was the unifying element in the La Guardia coalition. Republicans, Democrats, Socialists, and Mugwumps, Anglo-Saxons, Jews, and Italians—all had their particular grievances against the ruling machine, and in La Guardia these groups found an appropriate leader. A master of the politics of resentment, he had been expressing for decades the frustrations, angers, and exasperations of people who had been looking in on things from the outside.

But he was also a political leader who converted resentments into aspirations. An angry man, La Guardia had a vision: an alternative to government by discredited district leader. It isn't often that voters of a big city are offered a referendum of such importance. And if he catered to passion and prejudice and flung buckets of mud, as he had in the past, he also appealed to reason. One of his admirers, Professor Berle, has summed up the matter this way: La Guardia "could be and was a gut-fighter in New York politics," but "he knew the difference between gut-fighting and the society he hoped to create."[6]

And credit, too, to the men around La Guardia and his staff in the field. They created an organization almost overnight, co-ordinated it as well as was possible under the circumstances, arranged hundreds of meetings, prepared news releases and leaflets, solicited funds, answered the telephone, rang doorbells, policed the polls—they attended, in short, to the grubby but necessary details by which campaigns are won. Special credit goes, of course, to Seabury. He set the Tiger up. He chose La Guardia to make the kill. Together the Little Flower and the Mayflower prodded Gotham's conscience to throw out the ruling clique that had been misgoverning the city.

So, thanks to himself but also with the help of Seabury and the gratuitous aid of the dodos of Tammany Hall, La Guardia entered City Hall. The choice of a minority, he had received a conditional mandate. Whether he could consolidate his victory, and forge a wider political realignment against the united opposition he would face in 1937, would depend on how in the next four years he used the immense power he finally commanded.

APPENDIX

Official Results—New York City Mayoralty Election of 1933

I. Manhattan

ASSEMBLY DISTRICT	TOTAL VOTE	O'BRIEN VOTE	O'BRIEN %	MCKEE VOTE	MCKEE %	SOLOMON VOTE	SOLOMON %	LA GUARDIA REP. VOTE	LA GUARDIA REP. %	LA GUARDIA FUSION VOTE	LA GUARDIA FUSION %	LA GUARDIA TOTAL VOTE	LA GUARDIA TOTAL %
1. Lower Manhattan	18,801	9,874	52.51	2,033	10.81	402	2.13	3,428	18.23	2,864	15.23	6,292	33.46
2. Greenwich Village	17,503	7,906	45.16	1,175	6.71	311	1.77	4,584	26.18	3,331	19.03	7,915	45.21
3. Lower West Side	22,244	10,263	46.13	4,969	22.33	337	1.51	3,255	14.63	3,178	14.28	6,433	28.91
4. Lower East Side	13,395	5,333	39.81	4,332	32.34	367	2.73	1,849	13.80	1,238	9.24	3,087	23.04
5. Hell's Kitchen	20,324	12,615	62.06	3,398	16.71	247	1.21	2,391	11.76	1,584	7.79	3,975	19.55
6. Lower East Side	16,434	7,623	46.38	1,533	9.32	821	4.99	4,656	28.33	1,364	8.29	6,020	36.62
7. Central Park West	32,969	8,552	25.93	8,898	26.98	559	1.69	8,428	25.56	6,403	19.42	14,831	44.98
8. Lower East Side	16,026	5,820	36.31	2,573	16.05	620	3.86	3,571	22.28	2,838	17.70	6,409	39.98
9. Central Park West	32,776	8,963	27.34	8,768	26.75	599	1.82	7,021	21.42	7,263	22.15	14,284	43.57
10. Silk Stocking	24,913	5,788	23.23	5,635	22.61	414	1.66	7,101	28.50	5,713	22.93	12,814	51.43
11. Manhattanville	29,728	12,459	41.90	6,136	20.64	406	1.36	5,421	18.23	5,173	17.40	10,594	35.63

Manhattan (*continued*)

ASSEMBLY DISTRICT	TOTAL VOTE	O'BRIEN VOTE	O'BRIEN %	MCKEE VOTE	MCKEE %	SOLOMON VOTE	SOLOMON %	LA GUARDIA REP. VOTE	LA GUARDIA REP. %	LA GUARDIA FUSION VOTE	LA GUARDIA FUSION %	LA GUARDIA TOTAL VOTE	LA GUARDIA TOTAL %
12. Old Gashouse District	27,092	11,609	42.85	6,238	23.02	378	1.39	4,446	16.41	4,178	15.42	8,624	31.83
13. Morningside Heights	19,328	6,640	34.35	5,388	27.87	387	2.00	3,509	18.15	3,320	17.17	6,829	35.33
14. Yorkville	24,902	9,719	39.02	6,922	27.79	366	1.46	3,972	15.95	3,683	14.78	7,655	30.73
15. Central Park East	29,166	5,710	19.57	9,122	31.27	354	1.21	7,602	26.06	6,294	21.57	13,896	47.63
16. Yorkville	21,597	8,481	39.26	6,339	29.35	429	1.98	3,633	16.82	2,491	11.53	6,124	28.35
17. Spanish Harlem	15,356	5,392	35.11	4,837	31.49	320	2.08	2,325	15.14	2,101	13.68	4,426	28.82
18. East Harlem	23,614	7,438	31.49	2,664	11.28	548	2.32	7,261	30.74	5,498	23.28	12,759	54.02
19. Spanish Negro Harlem	17,245	6,677	38.71	3,606	20.91	441	2.55	4,457	25.84	1,876	10.87	6,333	36.71
20. East Harlem	14,515	4,212	29.01	2,461	16.95	345	2.37	3,463	23.85	3,887	26.77	7,350	50.62
21. Negro Harlem	21,290	6,374	29.93	6,020	28.27	362	1.70	5,597	26.28	2,837	13.32	8,434	39.60
22. Lower Washington Heights	23,856	9,077	38.04	6,032	25.28	452	1.89	4,456	18.67	3,686	15.45	8,142	34.12
23. Upper Washington Heights	52,466	16,124	30.73	14,628	27.88	1,060	2.02	9,776	18.63	10,477	19.96	20,253	38.59
TOTAL	535,520	192,649	35.97	123,707	23.10	10,525	1.96	112,202	20.95	91,277	17.04	203,479	37.99

II. Brooklyn

ASSEMBLY DISTRICT	TOTAL VOTE	O'BRIEN		MCKEE		SOLOMON		LA GUARDIA					
								REP.		FUSION		TOTAL	
		VOTE	%	VOTE	%	VOTE	%	VOTE	%	VOTE	%	VOTE	%
1. Brooklyn Heights	17,196	5,088	29.58	4,581	26.63	335	1.94	3,794	22.06	3,324	19.33	7,118	41.39
2. Coney Island, Sheepshead Bay, Flatlands, Midwood, Marine Park	97,533	24,576	25.19	24,754	25.38	4,332	4.44	19,812	20.31	22,135	22.69	41,947	43.00
3. South Brooklyn	13,895	4,894	35.22	3,360	24.18	199	1.43	2,579	18.56	2,769	19.92	5,348	38.48
4. Navy Yard	18,941	6,775	35.76	2,930	15.46	631	3.33	4,716	24.89	3,607	19.04	8,323	43.94
5. Stuyvesant Heights	22,355	5,975	26.72	6,841	30.60	600	2.68	6,021	26.93	2,823	12.62	8,844	39.55
6. Stuyvesant	19,338	5,748	29.72	3,280	16.96	1,386	7.16	5,571	28.80	3,007	15.54	8,578	44.35
7. Kensington	20,506	6,846	33.38	6,405	31.23	251	1.22	3,458	16.86	3,468	16.91	6,926	33.77
8. Gowanus	16,249	5,657	34.81	3,130	19.26	278	1.71	3,810	23.44	3,323	20.45	7,133	43.89
9. Bay Ridge	70,627	15,064	21.32	20,444	28.94	1,669	2.36	16,094	22.78	16,816	23.80	32,910	46.58
10. Park Slope	23,131	6,429	27.79	6,755	29.20	416	1.79	5,492	23.74	3,951	17.08	9,443	40.82
11. Crown Heights	30,962	8,001	25.84	8,651	27.94	745	2.40	7,526	24.30	5,857	18.91	13,383	43.21

Brooklyn (*continued*)

ASSEMBLY DISTRICT	TOTAL VOTE	O'BRIEN		MCKEE		SOLOMON		LA GUARDIA REP.		FUSION		TOTAL	
		VOTE	%	VOTE	%	VOTE	%	VOTE	%	VOTE	%	VOTE	%
12. Park Slope	28,152	9,385	33.33	8,729	31.00	565	2.00	5,487	19.49	3,857	13.70	9,344	33.19
13. Bushwick	14,602	4,092	28.02	2,547	17.44	380	2.60	3,799	26.01	3,620	24.79	7,419	50.80
14. Williamsburg	16,259	4,687	28.82	4,080	25.09	634	3.89	3,262	20.06	3,155	19.40	6,417	39.46
15. Greenpoint	15,569	5,920	38.02	5,968	38.33	186	1.19	1,922	12.34	1,537	9.87	3,459	22.21
16. Bensonhurst, Gravesend, Borough Park, Seagate	82,277	15,907	19.33	15,990	19.43	4,106	4.99	18,391	22.35	25,988	31.58	44,379	53.93
17. Bedford	22,430	5,535	24.67	6,416	28.60	749	3.33	6,048	26.96	3,503	15.61	9,551	42.57
18. East Flatbush	70,636	19,163	27.12	14,344	20.30	4,680	6.62	16,754	23.71	14,144	20.02	30,898	43.73
19. Bushwick	14,981	3,499	23.35	3,361	22.43	466	3.11	3,210	21.42	4,235	28.26	7,445	49.68
20. Ridgewood	28,586	6,556	22.93	10,148	35.49	505	1.76	6,237	21.81	5,018	17.55	11,255	39.36
21. Flatbush	55,952	12,881	23.02	15,017	26.83	1,551	2.77	14,226	25.42	11,930	21.32	26,156	46.74
22. East New York	41,300	8,020	19.41	12,671	30.68	2,051	4.96	9,763	23.63	8,057	19.50	17,820	43.13
23. Brownsville	17,507	3,637	20.77	4,156	23.73	1,226	7.00	3,595	20.53	4,229	24.15	7,824	44.68
TOTAL	758,984	194,335	25.60	194,558	25.63	26,941	3.54	171,567	22.60	160,353	21.12	331,920	43.72

Assembly Districts, New York County
(Manhattan)

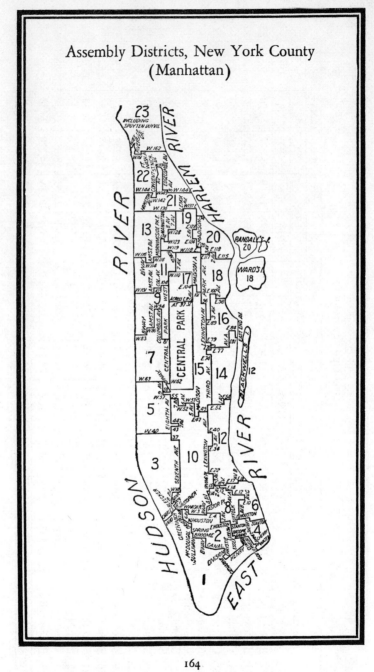

Assembly Districts, Kings County
(Brooklyn)

III. Bronx

ASSEMBLY DISTRICT	TOTAL VOTE	O'BRIEN		McKEE		SOLOMON		REP.		LA GUARDIA			
										FUSION		TOTAL	
		VOTE	%	VOTE	%	VOTE	%	VOTE	%	VOTE	%	VOTE	%
1. South Bronx	27,531	7,250	26.33	12,206	44.33	533	1.93	3,338	12.12	3,914	14.21	7,252	26.33
2. West Bronx	72,277	18,251	25.25	22,780	31.51	2,787	3.85	11,298	15.63	15,960	22.08	27,258	37.71
3. Hunt's Point	23,418	6,242	26.65	7,281	31.09	1,220	5.20	3,439	14.68	4,495	19.19	7,934	33.87
4. Morrisania, East of Prospect Avenue	20,945	6,456	30.82	6,401	30.56	1,047	4.99	2,647	12.63	3,495	16.68	6,142	29.31
5. Morrisania, West of Prospect Avenue	26,609	6,780	25.48	7,664	28.80	1,633	6.13	3,887	14.60	5,249	19.72	9,136	34.32
6. East Bronx	101,361	19,050	18.79	34,155	33.69	2,977	2.93	16,134	15.91	26,857	26.49	42,991	42.40
7. Tremont	29,873	6,306	21.10	6,496	21.74	1,518	5.08	4,863	16.27	9,408	31.49	14,271	47.76
8. Fordham Heights, Jerome Park Reservoir, Riverdale	98,086	23,068	23.51	34,297	34.96	3,043	3.10	15,248	15.54	21,437	21.85	36,685	37.39
TOTAL	400,100	93,403	23.34	131,280	32.81	14,758	3.68	60,854	15.20	90,815	22.69	151,669	37.89

Assembly Districts, Bronx County
(The Bronx)

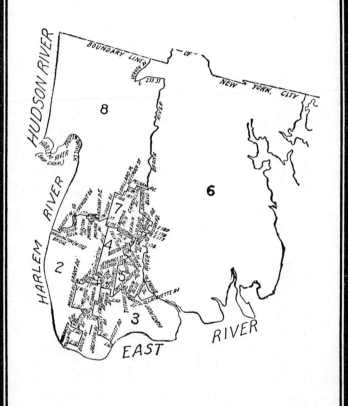

IV. Queens

ASSEMBLY DISTRICT	TOTAL VOTE	O'BRIEN		MCKEE		SOLOMON		LA GUARDIA					
								REP.		FUSION		TOTAL	
		VOTE	%	VOTE	%	VOTE	%	VOTE	%	VOTE	%	VOTE	%
1. Long Island City, Astoria	46,109	12,709	27.56	14,621	31.70	862	1.86	8,547	18.53	9,092	19.71	17,639	38.25
2. Sunnyside, Maspeth, Woodside-Winfield, Elmhurst, Nassau Heights	51,186	13,798	26.95	20,658	40.35	801	1.56	8,088	15.80	7,566	14.78	15,654	30.58
3. Jackson Heights, Corona, College Point, Whitestone	68,140	15,453	22.67	23,518	34.51	986	1.44	13,005	19.08	14,948	21.93	27,953	41.02
4. Jamaica East, Flushing	115,406	23,085	20.00	40,722	35.28	2,089	1.81	30,045	26.03	19,250	16.68	49,295	42.71
5. Jamaica West, Rockaways	70,699	17,303	24.47	24,255	34.30	1,414	2.00	16,542	23.39	10,985	15.53	27,527	38.93
6. Ridgewood, Glendale, Forest Hills	42,591	8,153	19.14	17,522	41.14	517	1.21	9,986	23.44	6,315	14.82	16,301	38.26
TOTAL	394,131	90,501	22.96	141,296	35.85	6,669	1.69	86,213	21.87	68,156	17.29	154,369	39.16

Assembly Districts, Queens County
(Queens)

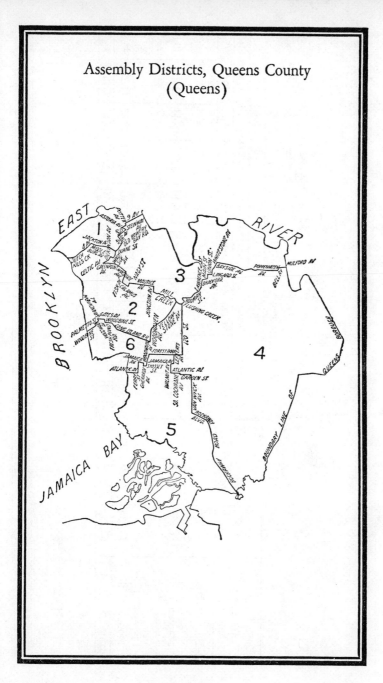

V. RICHMOND

| ASSEMBLY DISTRICT | TOTAL VOTE | O'BRIEN | | McKEE | | SOLOMON | | LA GUARDIA | | | | | |
| | | | | | | | | REP. | | FUSION | | TOTAL | |
		VOTE	%	VOTE	%	VOTE	%	VOTE	%	VOTE	%	VOTE	%
1. Port Richmond, Brighton, Stapleton	31,499	8,848	28.08	9,231	29.30	478	1.51	7,687	24.40	5,177	16.43	12,864	40.83
2. Tottenville, Prince's Bay, Great Kills, Dongan Hills	30,736	6,936	22.56	8,981	29.21	475	1.54	8,310	27.03	5,911	19.23	14,221	46.26
TOTAL	62,235	15,784	25.36	18,212	29.26	953	1.53	15,997	25.70	11,088	17.81	27,085	43.52

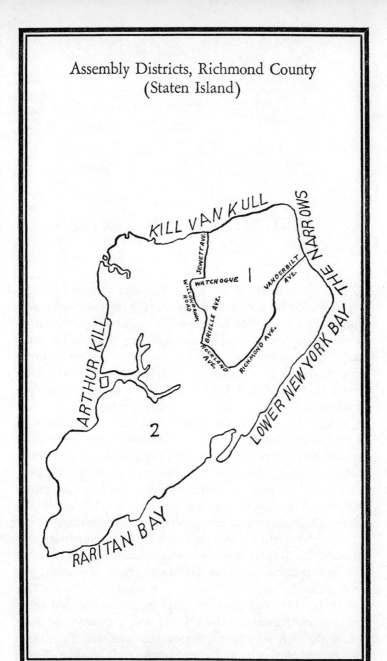

Assembly Districts, Richmond County
(Staten Island)

KILL VAN KULL

THE NARROWS

ARTHUR KILL

JEWETT AVE.
WATCHOGUE
WILLOWBROOK ROAD
BRIELLE AVE.
ROCKLAND AVE.
RICHMOND AVE.
VANDERBILT AVE.

1

2

LOWER NEW YORK BAY

RARITAN BAY

A Statement on Sources

The Notes to this book are so full that a formal bibliography would be not only repetitious but an exercise in pedantry. My general indebtedness to writers of American history is abundantly clear, and I have acknowledged in the footnotes only those works which clarified my understanding of problems in which La Guardia was directly involved. What remains to be said is a brief word about personal files, undocumented reminiscences, and election statistics.

The F. H. La Guardia Papers, stored in the Municipal Archives and Records Center, 238 William Street, New York, are the bibliographical backbone of this book. They contain correspondence, memoranda, newspaper clippings, congressional bills, campaign posters and leaflets, photographs, manuscripts and reprints of speeches and articles, press releases, La Guardia's public mayoralty papers, and a fragmentary draft of his incomplete autobiography. Stored in more than two hundred file drawers and nearly three hundred scrapbooks, his Papers constitute one of the largest collections of personal files in America.

Yet, however full, they left gaps in the record, and other personal collections to which I had access directly, or indirectly through friends, colleagues, and well-wishers, include the papers of Adolf A. Berle, Maurice P. Davidson, Lewis

Gannett, Joseph M. Price, Senator George Norris, Milo Reno, Frederick C. Tanner, Oswald Garrison Villard, Senator Robert F. Wagner, and Richard W. G. Welling. A further source of personal information came from the rich store of unpublished reminiscences that the Columbia University Oral History Project is still in the process of putting together. I found a dozen and more of those memoirs useful—Stanley Isaacs's and William Jay Schieffelin's particuarly so—and Paul Windels's was absolutely indispensable.

Like the Oral History autobiographies, the information I gained through interviews is undocumented. Having previously written other books and articles based partly on live evidence, I am fully aware of the danger involved in trusting unassisted memory. Yet it would be foolish as well as stuffy to turn down an opportunity because the historical handbooks are silent about sources available to writers of recent history. Talking with men and women who knew La Guardia, or reading their unpublished recollections, yielded lively anecdotes and also gave me a sense of contemporaneity with the past I otherwise might not have had. Furthermore, the tests that historians use to establish the probable authenticity of a primary source, internal consistency and corroborative evidence, are applicable to informal reminiscences. But all of us, not only scholars, are often forced to make decisions that can never be proven in black and white. The best safeguard in such cases is judgment based on an understanding of what fits a situation and what does not. The appended footnotes allow the reader to use his own judgment.

Several of the most revealing anecdotes in this book come from interviews and unpublished memoirs, but one may question the wisdom of quoting men who quote from memory what they or other men have said. Yet life happens anecdotally, and dialogue recaptures in all its liveliness and importance certain incidents in La Guardia's career. The important thing is not whether the words are recalled in their original order, which admittedly is most unlikely, but whether the meaning and flavor are authentic. I have not gone so far as one of the greatest of all narrative historians, Thucydides, in making up speeches, but I have followed his principle that man talking is often worth more than pages of extended narrative. The reading world is better off having Pericles' Funeral Oration as Thucydides heard it, or reconstructed it as others heard it, than having no Funeral Oration at all.

The *Annual Report of the Board of Elections in the City of New York* breaks down the official returns by county and assembly district, and the *City Record* by election district. But except for party registration, neither source identifies voters by economic status, ethnic background, religious affiliation, education, or other important variables. No source does, but it is possible to reconstruct *districts* according to some of those variables and, therefore, to read election returns against census returns. It is that kind of reading that I did in order to write most of Chapter V.

There are, happily, several books that have digested various parts of the enormous mass of data that the census takers collected about New York. Besides *New York City Market Analysis* (New York, 1933), compiled by the New York *Times, Herald Tribune,* and *News,* I found the statistical tables and maps particularly useful in the following: Godias J. Drolet, *et al., Health Center Districts, New York City, Handbook: Statistical Reference Data, Five-Year Period, 1929–1933* (New York, 1935); C. Morris Horowitz and Lawrence J. Kaplan, *The Jewish Population of the New York Area, 1900–1975* (New York, 1959); Walter Laidlaw, *Population of the City of New York, 1890–1930* (New York, 1932); William B. Shedd, "Italian Population in New York" (New York, undated); Mayor's Committee on City Planning, *Citywide Studies, Part I, Basic Factors in the Planning of the City of New York* (New York, 1940); Research Bureau, Welfare Council of New York City, *Homes by Tenure and Value or Monthly Rental, by Health Areas, New York City, 1930* (New York, 1933); Research Bureau, Welfare Council of New York City, *Population in Health Areas, New York City, 1930* (New York, 1931); Research Bureau, Welfare Council of New York City, *Heads of Families by Color and Nativity and Country of Birth of Foreign Born Head, by Health Areas* (New York, 1934).

For some inexplicable reason, unless it means to be unkind to historians, the Board of Elections does not include county, assembly district, or election district maps in its reports. Happily, the Municipal Reference Library of New York City has such maps for the years concerned in this book. They are different in scale from the census maps and also in their basic units (election district versus census tract), but it is possible to correlate the two sets of maps. The result of the correlation is the transformation of an assembly or election district designated by an impersonal number into a community, or communities, of people with identifiable characteristics. And only after identifying voters can one ask and try to answer the question: who voted for whom and why?

Notes

To avoid distracting and wearying the reader with fre-
quent citations, I have followed the now common practice
of combining the references in a single note for a pas-
sage. The F. H. La Guardia Papers have been abbreviated
as LGP.

CHAPTER I

"Now We Have a Mayor of New York!"

1. New York *Times*, January 1, 1934.

2. *A B C Weekly*, February 1, 1941; Robert Moses, *La Guardia,
A Salute and a Memoir* (New York, 1957), 30; press release, April
21, 1958, from Maurice G. Postley for the La Guardia Memorial
Association. Two stained-glass windows, installed in La Guardia's
honor at Christ Episcopal Church in Riverdale, New York, in 1958,
portray the following saints: St. Francis of Assisi, who, according
to the press release, "typifies kindness and humanitarian qualities";
and St. Michael, the winged warrior, recalling La Guardia's war-
time service as an aviator. La Guardia attended the church during
the last years of his life.

3. *Yale Alumni Magazine* (July 12, 1940), 15.

4. Interview with Edward Corsi, New York City, December
27, 28, 1956.

5. New York *Times*, January 1, 1934.

6. Mrs. Marie F. La Guardia, *Reminiscences* (Oral History
Project, Columbia University, 1950), 17; New York *Times*, January 1, 1934.

7. Quoted in Rebecca B. Rankin, ed., *New York Advancing: A Scientific Approach to Municipal Government, 1934–1935* (New York, 1936), ii.

8. New York *Times*, January 2, 3, 1934; New York *American*, January 3, 1934; New York *Daily News*, January 3, 1934; Brooklyn *Times Union*, January 2, 1934; New York *Herald Tribune*, January 1, 1934.

9. Cleveland Rodgers, Rebecca B. Rankin, *New York: The World's Capital* (New York, 1948), 114, 119–120. For the quotation, "I seen my opportunities and I took 'em"—and the philosophy that lay behind the quotation—see *Plunkitt of Tammany Hall*, recorded by William L. Riordon, introduction by Arthur Mann (New York, 1963), 3, vii–xxii, and *passim*.

10. For the details concerning La Guardia's hybrid background, see Arthur Mann, *La Guardia, A Fighter Against His Times, 1882–1933* (Philadelphia, 1959), 19–42, 100, 237, 246–256, and *passim*.

11. For a splendid account of the pluralist pressures on those who govern New York City, see Wallace S. Sayre, Herbert Kaufman, *Governing New York City* (New York, 1960), 39 ff.

12. Frank Dyer Chester to Robert Bacon, January 17, 1906, *Consular Dispatches*, vol. IV, Records of the Department of State, Record Group 59, National Archives; memorandum by La Guardia, enclosed with Chester to Bacon, March 8, 1906, *ibid.*

13. New York *Times*, May 4, 1918.

14. *Nowy Swiat*, November 6, 1942; interview with Paul Windels, New York City, summer, 1956.

15. Interview with Joey Adams, New York City, December 13, 1958.

16. Quoted in Charles Garrett, *The La Guardia Years, Machine and Reform Politics in New York City* (New Brunswick, 1961), 123.

17. Charles Culp Burlingham, *Reminiscences* (Oral History Project, Columbia University, 1961), 34.

18. Edward J. Flynn, *You're the Boss* (New York, 1947), 138.

19. Interview with Mrs. Gemma La Guardia Gluck, La Guardia's sister, Long Island City, N.Y., July 19, 1956.

20. For the titles in La Guardia's personal library in 1933, see "Books Sent to 1274 Fifth Avenue," LGP.

21. Walter Johnson, *William Allen White's America* (New York, 1947), 466–467. For other expressions concerning La Guardia and the Presidency, see New York *Times*, November 4, 7, 21, 1937; *Current History*, XLVII (December, 1937), 16–17; Karl Schriftgiesser, "Portrait of a Mayor, Fiorello La Guardia," *Atlantic Monthly*, CLXI (January, 1938), 63; *Fortune*, XVII (January, 1938), 92; John Chamberlain, "Mayor La Guardia," *Yale Review*, XXIX (September, 1939), 27; C. B. Yorke to La Guardia, Decem-

ber 20, 1937, LGP; Eugene M. Elliott to La Guardia, March 24, 1938, *Ibid.;* La Guardia to Elliott, April 4, 1938, *Ibid.* For Tugwell's tribute to La Guardia, see his review of the first volume of this biography in the New York *Times* book review section of Sunday, November 15, 1959, and his *The Art of Politics, as Practiced by Three Great Americans: Franklin Delano Roosevelt, Luis Muñoz Marin, and Fiorello H. La Guardia* (Garden City, 1958).

22. Quoted in Duff Gilfond, "La Guardia of Harlem," *American Mercury*, XI (June, 1927), 155.

23. New York *Herald Tribune*, July 6, 1924.

24. New York *Times*, September 26, 1926; *Congressional Record*, 69 Cong., Sess. 1, 2010–2012, 2135.

CHAPTER II

The Little Flower and the Mayflower

1. For these and other biographical details, I have relied primarily on Herbert Mitgang, *The Man Who Rode the Tiger, The Life and Times of Judge Samuel Seabury* (Philadelphia, 1963), the best and most recent study, and also on the older but still useful *Samuel Seabury: A Challenge* (New York, 1932), by Walter Chambers.

2. Quoted in M. W. Werner, *Tammany Hall* (New York, 1928), 441.

3. For the response of the New York gentry to boss politics in the late nineteenth century, see Theodore Roosevelt, *An Autobiography* (New York, 1926), 59; Richard Welling, *As the Twig Is Bent* (New York, 1942), 40 ff; Elting E. Morison, *Turmoil and Tradition, A Study of the Life and Times of Henry L. Stimson* (New York, 1964), 61–74; John Morton Blum, *The Republican Roosevelt* (New York, 1962), 7–36; Charles Garrett, *The La Guardia Years, Machine and Reform Politics in New York City* (New Brunswick, 1961), 20–47. On the number and range of Good Government organizations, see Clifford W. Patton, *The Battle for Municipal Reform* (Washington, 1940), 34–44; William H. Tolman, *Municipal Reform Movements in the United States* (New York, 1895).

4. Quoted in Chambers, *Seabury*, 180.

5. Quoted in Mitgang, *The Man Who Rode the Tiger*, 118.

6. La Guardia to Frederick C. Tanner, August 13, 1913, in the possession of Tanner.

7. *Literary Digest*, CXVI (September 2, 1933), 7.

8. Quoted in Arthur Mann, *La Guardia, A Fighter Against His Times, 1882–1933* (Philadelphia, 1959), 276–277.

9. William B. Northrop, John B. Northrop, *The Insolence of Office: The Story of the Seabury Investigations* (New York, 1932) is the most detailed account of the background and course of the monumental inquest that bears Seabury's name.

10. *Newsweek*, LXI (May 19, 1958), 35.

11. Quoted in Mitgang, *The Man Who Rode the Tiger*, 157.

12. There is as yet no satisfactory history of Tammany, but the best and fullest account is M. W. Werner's *Tammany Hall* (New York, 1928). On the decline of the gentry and the rise of the professional politician, see Robert V. Remini, *The Election of Andrew Jackson* (Philadelphia, 1963), an illuminating analysis. *Cf.* M. I. Ostrogorski, *Democracy and the Organization of Political Parties* (New York, 1902), vol. II, 66–71, 149–225, 367–440, 459–483; James Bryce, *American Commonwealth* (New York, 1912), vol. II, 56–175, 379–405. For a defense of the organization at its height, see *Plunkitt of Tammany Hall* (New York, 1963), and when it was on the defensive, Edward J. Flynn, *You're the Boss* (New York, 1947), particularly 219–235. For the role of the Irish in the machine, compare the account in Nathan Glazer and Daniel P. Moynihan, *Beyond the Melting Pot* (New York, 1963), 217–229, with that of William V. Shannon in *The American Irish* (New York, 1963), 1–85, 131–181. There is a particularly good description of the structure of the Democratic organization on the eve of the 1933 election in Roy V. Peel, "The Political Machine of New York City," *American Political Science Review*, XXVII (August, 1933), 611–618. For an illuminating analysis of the machine before the Seabury investigations, see Joseph McGoldrick, "The New Tammany," *American Mercury*, XV (September, 1928), 1–12.

13. Quoted in Milton Mackaye, *The Tin Box Parade: A Handbook for Larceny* (New York, 1934), 306.

14. Quoted in John Dewey, *New York and the Seabury Investigation* (2nd edition: New York, 1933), 10.

15. Quoted in Mitgang, *The Man Who Rode the Tiger*, 233.

16. Quoted in Mackaye, *The Tin Box Parade*, 305.

17. Quoted in Chambers, *Seabury*, 354.

18. Dewey, *New York and the Seabury Investigation*, 14–16.

19. Quoted in Julius S. Mason, "The Scandals of New York," *Current History*, XXXVI (August, 1932), 529.

20. For the testimony of McCormick, McQuade, and Farley, see Mackaye, *The Tin Box Parade*, 194–196, 201–202, 208; Chambers, *Seabury*, 338.

21. Mitgang, *The Man Who Rode the Tiger*, 162–163, 240–241, 242.

22. Quoted in Warren Moscow, "Plea for Paying for Politicking," New York *Times Magazine* (October 22, 1961), 90. On Doyle's practice, see Mitgang, *The Man Who Rode the Tiger*, 223.

23. Quoted in Mitgang, *The Man Who Rode the Tiger*, 226.

24. Garrett, *The La Guardia Years*, 74.

25. Quoted in *Final Report of Samuel Seabury, Referee to the Supreme Court, Appellate Division—First Department* (March 28, 1932), 36.

26. Quoted in Northrop and Northrop, *The Insolence of Office*, 53.

27. Mitgang, *The Man Who Rode the Tiger*, 191–193; Dewey, *New York and the Seabury Investigation*, 37.

28. Quoted in Gene Fowler, *The Life & Times of Jimmy Walker, Beau James* (New York, 1949), 379.

29. The quotations, in the order of their appearance, are taken from Mitgang, *The Man Who Rode the Tiger*, 169; *Time* LXXI (May 19, 1958), 17; Fowler, *The Life & Times of Jimmy Walker*, 302, 312.

30. Raymond Moley, *27 Masters of Politics, In a Personal Perspective* (New York, 1949), 208.

31. The full charges against Walker by Seabury are contained in an appendix to Norman Thomas and Paul Blanshard, *What's The Matter With New York* (New York, 1932), 350–355. The New York *Times*, May 26–27, 1932, contains a full transcript of Walker's testimony, with his witticisms of the two days.

32. Quoted in Mitgang, *The Man Who Rode the Tiger*, 296.

33. Quoted in Ernest Cuneo, *Life With Fiorello* (New York, 1955), 186.

34. *Time*, XXI (January 30, 1933), 15.

35. *Time*, XXII (July 10, 1933), 13.

36. *Annual Report of the Board of Elections in the City of New York for the Year 1932* (New York, 1933), 46, 49, 82.

37. New York *Times*, August 30, 1930; *Time*, XXII (August 14, 1933), 14.

CHAPTER III

Nomination After Midnight

1. La Guardia to Villard, November 22, 1932, Oswald Garrison Villard Papers, Houghton Library, Harvard University.

2. For biographical details about the four men, one is limited to the following: on Davidson, his obituary in the New York *Times*, July 17, 1956; on Whitman, *National Cyclopaedia of American Biography* (New York, 1947), vol. XXXIII, 17; on Smull, *ibid.*, (1934), current volume D, 292; on Price, *ibid.* (1951), vol. XXXVII, 371.

3. William Jay Schieffelin, "New York City Cleans House,"

Review of Reviews, LXXXIII (May, 1931), 49; Maurice P. Davidson, "The Redemption of New York City," printed Address at the Town Meeting, Philadelphia, Pa., November 20, 1938, M. P. Davidson Papers, 730 Fifth Avenue, New York City; "Statement of Purposes and Declaration of Principles of the City Party," November 26, 1932, a printed leaflet, *ibid.*

4. Interview with Edward Corsi, New York City, March 31, 1960.

5. Sally Peters to Richard Welling, October 26, 1933, Richard W. G. Welling Papers, Manuscript Division, New York Public Library. Hereafter referred to as Welling Papers.

6. Samuel S. Koenig, *Reminiscences* (Oral History Project, Columbia University, 1950), 45; *Voters Directory*, a special number of the *Searchlight*, XIX (October, 1929), 4.

7. La Guardia to John Gerdes, September 19, 1933, LGP.

8. Lewis Gannett, "Books and Other Things," New York *Herald Tribune*, March 12, 1931; La Guardia to Gannett, March 16, 1931, Lewis Gannett Papers in the possession of Mr. Gannett; Gannett to La Guardia, March 18, 1931, *ibid.*; La Guardia to Gannett, March 21, 1931, *ibid.*

9. Of all the accounts of McKee, the one that tries hardest to be objective is *Time*, XXII (October 23, 1933), 13.

10. Interview with Adolf A. Berle, New York City, March 29, 1960.

11. For the circumstances of La Guardia's meeting Berle, and their collaboration in Congress, see Arthur Mann, *La Guardia, A Fighter Against His Times, 1882–1933* (Philadelphia, 1959), 323–326.

12. Interview with Berle, *supra*. Burlingham died in 1959, and there is as yet no adequate biography of him even in the form of an article. The most detailed account is in *National Cyclopaedia of American Biography* (New York, 1938), current volume E, 1937–1938, 295.

13. New York *Times*, May 4, 8, 11, 15, 20, 1933.

14. New York *Times*, March 25, 28, May 11, 18, 22, June 6, 1933.

15. La Guardia to James Marshall, May 26, 1933, LGP.

16. Newbold Morris, *Let the Chips Fall: My Battles Against Corruption* (New York, 1955), 58–72; Morris to La Guardia, May 15, 1933, LGP.

17. La Guardia to Courtlandt Nicoll, May 18, 1933, LGP.

18. Morris, *Let the Chips Fall*, 87–88.

19. New York *Times*, May 20, 1933.

20. Stanley M. Isaacs, *Reminiscences* (Oral History Project, Columbia University, 1956), 72.

21. Chase Mellen, Jr., "Memorandum to Arthur Mann, North-

ampton, Mass., re 1933 New York County Primary Campaign,"
July 30, 1959.

22. Interview with Corsi, *supra*.

23. Interview with W. Kingsland Macy, Babylon, Long Island,
September 14, 1959.

24. Wallace S. Sayre to Samuel Seabury, July 18, 1933, carbon
enclosed with Sayre to La Guardia, July 18, 1933, LGP.

25. Maurice P. Davidson, "Wanted: A Mayor," undated manuscript, Davidson Papers; Joseph D. McGoldrick, "A Farewell to
Tammany," *Independent Journal of Columbia University*, II (November 1, 1933), I, 3.

26. Maurice P. Davidson, "Interview as Recorded," with Gerard
H. Silverburgh (manuscript, 1953), 24–25, 34, Davidson Papers.

27. Quoted in Herbert Mitgang, *The Man Who Rode the Tiger,
The Life and Times of Judge Samuel Seabury* (New York, 1963),
313.

28. La Guardia to C. C. Burlingham, April 13, 1943, LGP.

29. M. L. Ernst to C. C. Burlingham, October 6, 1933, LGP.

30. Rufus E. McGahen to Arthur Mann, July 15, 1959.

31. The Burlingham-Welling-Howe exchanges are in the Welling Papers.

32. Joseph M. Price to Richard Welling, July 18, 1933, Welling
Papers. *Cf.* Cleveland Rodgers, *Robert Moses, Builder for Democracy* (New York, 1952), 79; Press Statement (unreleased and undated but probably in July, 1933), "Statement of Reason for
Joseph M. Price's Withdrawal from Fusion Conference: Judge
Seabury's Objections to Robert Moses's Availability as Mayoralty
Candidate," Joseph M. Price Papers, Columbia University Libraries; Robert Moses to Joseph M. Price, July 29, 1933, *ibid.*

33. Quoted in Davidson, "Interview as Recorded," 26.

34. New York *Times*, July 27, 1933.

35. Interview with Robert Moses, Babylon, Long Island, September 14, 1959.

36. C. C. Burlingham to Richard Welling, August 18, 1933,
Davidson Papers.

37. John F. O'Ryan to Richard Welling, August 3, 1933, Welling
Papers.

38. New York *Times*, July 28, 29, 1933.

39. Charles C. Burlingham, "Nomination of Fiorello H. La
Guardia for Mayor of the City of New York in 1933" (pamphlet,
1943), 3; New York *Times*, August 3, 4, 1933.

40. Interview with Berle, *supra*.

41. New York *Times*, August 4, 1933; Interviews with Corsi,
supra, and Charles H. Tuttle, New York City, March 30, 1960.

42. Quoted in New York *Times*, August 4, 1933. In reconstructing the Bar Association meeting, I have relied on the August 4 issue

of the *Times;* Interview with Berle, *supra;* Davidson, "Interview as Recorded," 30–32; William J. Schieffelin to Richard Welling, August 22, 1933, Welling Papers; Schieffelin, *Reminiscences* (Oral History Project, Columbia University, 1949), 42–43.

43. Quoted in Paul J. Kern, "Fiorello H. La Guardia," in J. T. Salter, ed., *The American Politician* (Chapel Hill, 1938), 18.

CHAPTER IV

The Campaign of 1933

1. Edward J. Flynn, *You're the Boss* (New York, 1947), 133.
2. Alva Johnston, "The Scholar in Politics–I," *New Yorker,* XLIX (July 1, 1933), 18; Johnston, "The Scholar In Politics–II," *ibid.,* XLIX (July 8, 1933), 17, 18, 19; Milton Mackaye, *The Tin Box Parade* (New York, 1934), 324; Allen Raymond, "From Playboy to Pietist," *North American Review,* CCXXXV (January, 1933), 6; Robert S. Allen, ed., *Our Fair City* (New York, 1947), 49.
3. La Guardia to Foreign Language Newspapers, September 23, 1933, LGP; La Guardia to William M. Calder, September 5, 1933, *ibid.;* Calder to La Guardia, August 28, 1933, *ibid.;* New York *Times,* September 15, 1933.
4. *The Fusion Handbook* (New York, 1933), 132–152; "For District Attorney Jacob Gould Schurman, Jr., Fusion Candidate" (Fusion leaflet), in Smith College Collection, *Documents Relating to the Fusion Campaign of 1933.* Hereafter referred to as Smith College Collection.
5. Interview with Joseph D. McGoldrick, Brooklyn, N. Y., April 1, 1961.
6. New York *Times,* September 20, 22, 1933; *Time,* XXII (October 2, 1933), 13; Chase Mellen, Jr., to La Guardia, undated, 1933, LGP.
7. *Literary Digest,* CXVI (October 7, 1933), 9.
8. Flynn, *You're the Boss,* 133; James A. Farley, *Jim Farley's Story: The Roosevelt Years* (New York, 1948), 42–43; New York *Times,* September 23, 24, 25, 26, 27, 29, 30, October 3, 1933; Stanley M. Isaacs to La Guardia, September 25, 1933, LGP; George U. Harvey to Joseph V. McKee, September 26, 1933, *ibid.;* La Guardia to Harvey, September 26, *ibid.*
9. James M. Burns, *Roosevelt: The Lion and the Fox* (New York, 1956), 377.
10. Flynn, *You're the Boss,* 132–133; Farley, *Jim Farley's Story,* 42–43.
11. "Because some thought that Roosevelt backed McKee, we suffered some losses. Nathan Straus, for instance, proposed for a

place on the Fusion ticket, pulled out and joined the McKee ticket instead." Adolf A. Berle to Arthur Mann, April 23, 1965.

12. Paul Windels, *Reminiscences* (Oral History Project, Columbia University, 1949–1950), Appendix (added in 1953), 1–3; Charles Culp Burlingham, *Reminiscences* (Oral History Project, Columbia University, 1961), 33.

13. Flynn, *You're the Boss*, 135–136; Windels, *Reminiscences*, 80, Appendix, 14.

14. New York *Times*, October 9, 10, 11, 1933; *Nation*, CXXXVII (October 25, 1933), 472.

15. Marie G. Gueringer to La Guardia, September 18, 1933, LGP. The La Guardia papers bulge with correspondence concerning the activities of Italo-Americans in the campaign. See, for example, La Guardia to Mrs. L. Perera, August 23, 1933; Matthew Benvenuto, *et al.*, to La Guardia, December 9, 1933; William Chadbourne to Marcantonio, November 5, 1933; Lucy Lotito to La Guardia, October 21, 1933; Vincenzo Patula to La Guardia, October 6, 1933; La Guardia to Patula, October 7, 1933; Nicholas H. Pinto to La Guardia, September 13, 1933; La Guardia to Pinto, September 15, 1933; Anthony P. Savarese to La Guardia, September 15, 1933; La Guardia to Savarese, September 16, 1933; Savarese to Edward Corsi, October 2, 1933; Ralph Senese to Paul Windels, December 12, 1933; O. H. Zeuli to La Guardia, October 23, 1933, LGP.

16. Quoted in mimeographed Bulletin No. 2 of Fusioneers, October 16, 1933, LGP. For Holmes's request, see John Haynes Holmes to George J. Abrams, October 24, 1933, *ibid.* There is an interesting account of the Honest Ballot Association in Eleanor Ernst, "Fusion Campaign Methods in the New York Fusion Mayoralty Campaign of 1933" (Smith College honors thesis, 1934), 93–98.

17. For La Guardia's explosion and the way his campaign manager soothed him, see, respectively, La Guardia to William M. Chadbourne, September 14, 1933, LGP; Charles Garrett, *The La Guardia Years, Machine and Reform Politics in New York City* (New Brunswick, 1961), 107. On the character and also the difficulties of the La Guardia organization, see Fusion Headquarters to La Guardia, October 23, 1933, LGP; Fusion Campaign Manager for Manhattan to I. V. Cook, October 24, 1933, *ibid.*; W. Ward Smith to La Guardia, October 29, 1933, *ibid.*

18. "Statement to the Press on Registration by Major La Guardia" (press release, undated) LGP; "Remember Registration Week" (printed instructions sheet to Fusion field workers from Ben Howe, Director of Organization), *ibid.*; "Plan of Organization for Assembly and Election Districts for Fusion Campaign" (printed Fusion instructions sheet), *ibid.*; *Annual Report of the*

Board of Elections in the City of New York for the Year 1933 (New York, 1934), 42; Ernst, "Fusion Campaign Methods," 93.

19. Windels, *Reminiscences*, Appendix, 4.

20. Interview with Edward Corsi, New York City, March 31, 1960. For wealthy Republican contributors, see Ernst, "Fusion Campaign Methods," 43.

21. Quoted in Daniel Bell, "Crime as an American Way of Life," *Antioch Review*, XIII (Summer, 1953), 149.

22. William D. Bosler to La Guardia, September 2, 1933, LGP.

23. Paul Blanshard to La Guardia, October 4, 1933, LGP.

24. New York *Times*, October 3, 1933.

25. Press release, October 29, 1933, LGP. The two preceding quotations come, respectively, from New York *Times*, October 11, 1933; A La Guardia speech (typewritten copy, undated), beginning with the words, "On the eve of the election . . .," LGP.

26. New York *Times*, October 21, 1933; August 2, 1929.

27. "Acceptance Speech by Joseph V. McKee" (Cooper Union Hall, October 11, 1933), 5–6, Smith College Collection; F. H. La Guardia, "McKee's Campaign Speech and McKee's Official Record" (manuscript, October 13, 1933), LGP.

28. "Address of Prof. A. A. Berle at Cooper Union, Monday, October 2, 1933" (mimeographed), LGP; New York *Times*, October 3, 1933.

29. Walter Lippmann, "Today *and* Tomorrow: The Issues in New York City," *Enquirer*, November 1, 1933.

30. Ernst, "Fusion Campaign Methods," 55–56; "Voters Directory," a special number of *The Searchlight*, XXIII (October, 1933), 4.

31. Rebecca B. Rankin, ed., *New York Advancing, A Scientific Approach to Municipal Government, 1934–1935* (New York, 1936), 198, 343.

32. "Memorandum for address of F. H. La Guardia on Social Justice" (typescript), LGP.

33. *Ibid.*

34. Roger N. Baldwin to La Guardia, August 25, 1933, LGP.

35. Paul Blanshard, "La Guardia Versus McKee," *Nation*, CXXXVII (October 25, 1933), 477. See also Oswald Garrison Villard, "Issues and Men, Fiorello H. La Guardia," *ibid.*, CXXXVII (August 30, 1933), 231.

36. La Guardia to Oswald Garrison Villard, August 30, 1933, LGP.

37. For a perceptive account of the mood of Italo-Americans in the fall of 1933, see the Brooklyn *Times Union*, October 31, 1933. The quotations come, respectively, from Patrick S. Hickey to La Guardia, September 25, 1933, LGP; New York *Times*, October 7, 1933.

38. Johnston, "The Scholar in Politics—II," *loc. cit.*, 18; Interview with Corsi, *supra; Il Progresso Italo-Americano,* November 5, 1933; New York *Amsterdam News,* November 1, 1933; *Jewish Morning Journal,* November 6, 1933; Konrad Furubotn to Paul Windels, November 25, 1933, LGP; William Farkas to La Guardia, October 30, 1933, *ibid.;* La Guardia to Farkas, October 31, 1933, *ibid.;* René H. Carsten to La Guardia, November 4, 1933, *ibid.*

39. Speech to the Puerto Ricans (typescript, undated), LGP; New York *Times,* November 6, 1933.

40. Robert Moses, *La Guardia, A Salute and a Memoir* (New York, 1957), 37–38.

41. H. Thebald to La Guardia, August 5, 1933, LGP.

42. Windels, *Reminiscences,* Appendix, 14–17, is the fullest behind-the-scenes account of the anti-Semitic incident. The quotations come from page 17.

43. New York *Times,* October 15, 1933.

44. Joseph Vincent McKee, "A Serious Problem," *Catholic World,* CI (May, 1915), 210–212. The full text of McKee's 1915 article was reprinted in the October 17, 1933, New York *Times* issue.

45. New York *Times,* October 16, 1933.

46. Flynn, *You're the Boss,* 137; "A Straightforward Answer to a 'Scurrilous Libel' " (radio address by Joseph V. McKee), 4, Smith College Collection.

47. New York *Times,* October 17, 18, 20, 1933; *American Hebrew and Jewish Tribune,* CXXXIII (November 3, 1933), 405.

48. See the following articles by McKee in the *Catholic World:* "Shall Women Vote?" CII (October, 1915), 45–54; "The Gary System," CII (January, 1916), 508–516; "The Latin American Congress," CII (March, 1916), 811–819; "The Charities Investigation," CIII (April, 1916), 87–97; "The Call of the Child," CIV (January, 1917), 523–532; "The Failure of Modern Education," CV (April, 1917), 1–11; "The Anomaly of Modern Education," CV (September, 1917), 721–731; "The Paradox of History," CVI (October, 1917), 82–90; "Woman and Child Labor Under War Conditions," CVI (March, 1918), 742–751.

49. New York *Times,* October 22, 23, 25, 26, 1933; "La Guardia Unmasked, Proof of His Affiliation with Communistic Organizations" (printed address by Joseph V. McKee), Smith College Collection; "Let Us Look at the Record: A Few Cold Facts about a Republican-Progressive-Socialist-Fusionist" (Recovery poster), *ibid.*

50. Flynn, *You're the Boss,* 137–138.

51. Norman Thomas to Dear Friend, October 5, 1933 (Socialist leaflet in the form of an open letter), LGP; *Weekly People,* November 4, 1933; "What Is Fusion?" (Communist Party leaflet, 1933), LGP.

52. Maurice Deutsch to La Guardia, October 27, 1933, LGP; La Guardia to Deutsch, October 30, 1933, LGP.

53. Quoted in unidentified newspaper clipping, Scrap Book of 1933 Campaign, LGP.

54. Lowell M. Limpus, Burr W. Leyson, *This Man La Guardia* (New York, 1938), 372–374.

55. New York *Times,* November 8, 1933.

56. Judge Eugene R. Canudo, who was co-chairman of the Fusioneers in Brooklyn, has written (Canudo to Arthur Mann, April 21, 1965): "I was in the field that day [Election Day], all over Brooklyn (Adonis' home town) and I don't remember seeing any of these gangsters on our side."

57. Quoted in Walter S. Mack, Jr., *Reminiscences* (Oral History Project, Columbia University, 1950), 47. For the quotation immediately preceding, see New York *Times,* November 8, 1933.

58. New York *World-Telegram,* November 8, 1933; New York *Times,* November 8, 1933; *Annual Report of the Board of Elections in the City of New York for the Year 1933* (New York, 1934), 56–57.

59. Except for the quotation from La Guardia's Arizona teacher, which comes from the New York *Times,* November 9, 1933, the others are culled from the LGP.

60. Quoted in New York *Evening Journal,* November 8, 1933.

CHAPTER V

A Crazy-Quilt Coalition

1. According to La Guardia's research staff, there were 3,651,-934 native-born and naturalized citizens of voting age in New York City in 1931. (See Ralph Hilton to La Guardia, September 26, 1933, and undated press release, 1933, "Statement to the Press on Registration by Major La Guardia," LGP.) La Guardia's 868,-522 return was 23.77 per cent of 3,651,934.

2. See, for example, Edward C. Banfield, James Q. Wilson, *City Politics* (Cambridge, 1963), the most recent book about the variables in voting behavior. Cf. Bernard Berelson, *et al., Voting* (Chicago, 1954); Angus Campbell, *The American Voter* (New York, 1960); Campbell, *et al., The Voter Decides* (Evanston, 1954); Robert A. Dahl, *Who Governs?* (New Haven, 1961); V. O. Key, Jr., *Public Opinion and American Democracy* (New York, 1961); Paul F. Lazarsfeld, *et al., The Peoples' Choice* (New York, 1944); Seymour M. Lipset, *Political Man* (New York, 1960); Samuel Lubell, *The Future of American Politics* (New York, 1952); Theodore H. White, *The Making of the President 1960* (New York, 1962), especially 213–243.

3. Godias J. Drolet, *et al.*, *Health Center Districts, New York City, Handbook: Statistical Reference Data, Five-Year Period, 1929–1933* (New York, 1935), 41–42; *New York City Market Analysis*, compiled jointly by the New York *Herald Tribune*, *News,* and *Times* (New York, 1933), "City Composite" (this book is unpaginated, and hereafter citations will be made according to the heading of the sheet); Walter Laidlaw, *Population of the City of New York, 1890–1930* (New York, 1932), 275.

4. The percentages are based on the returns for the Republican Hoover in the Presidential election of 1932, and are higher than the figures for Republican registration in the districts in question (the Seventh, Ninth, Fifteenth, Eighteenth and Twenty-first Assembly Districts in Manhattan, and the Ninth and Seventeenth Assembly Districts in Brooklyn). For a comparison between the registration figures and voting returns in numbers, from which the percentages are derived, see *Annual Report of the Board of Elections in the City of New York for the Year 1932* (New York, 1933), 40–43, 46–47.

5. *Ibid.*, 46.

6. *Annual Report of the Board of Elections in the City of New York for the Year 1933* (New York, 1934), 56–57.

7. These percentages are based on the official returns in the *Annual Report of the Board of Elections in the City of New York* for the years 1928, 1932, and 1933. Like all other percentages throughout this chapter, these are derived from the following

formula: $\dfrac{\text{return for the candidate by area in question}}{\text{total votes recorded on the public counter } minus \text{ unrecorded in area in question}}$

The unrecorded column in the official return is a tally of abstentions and invalidated ballots.

8. Interview with Francis R. Stoddard, New York City, November 23, 1955.

9. At a moment like this, the historian can only envy the contemporary election analyst, who is able to sample a live electorate and poll it. In the absence of that technique, one must improvise as best one can. Two ways suggest themselves: (1) In order to arrive at a not unreasonable estimate of La Guardia's percentage of Hoover's vote, let us take the Fifteenth Assembly District, the most Republican in the city, and divide La Guardia's return by Hoover's, $\dfrac{13,896}{16,742}.$ The quotient comes out to 83 per cent. Now, Hoover's city-wide return was 584,056, and 83 per cent of it is 484,766. The latter figure was La Guardia's probable and approximate share of Hoover's vote; (2) Let us take La

Notes 189

Guardia's total return and subtract from it the approximate number of votes he probably got but Hoover most likely did not: Thus

868,522 (La Guardia's total return)

−260,451 (A Democratic vote: the difference between Roosevelt's and the joint McKee-O'Brien returns)

− 63,846 (A Socialist vote: the difference between Norman Thomas's Presidential return in 1932 and Charles Solomon's—La Guardia's opponent)

_____

544,225

But one must subtract from the latter figure an estimated 40,000 Italo-Americans who voted in 1933 but not in 1932, and also an unknown number of independents and of New Yorkers who reached voting age after 1932 and voted for the first time in 1933. As in the first method, the return for La Guardia of Hoover's vote falls between 450,000 and 500,000.

10. See, for example, Drolet, *Health Center Districts*, 91 ff; and the sheets for the districts in question in *New York City Market Analysis*.

11. "Official Canvass of the Votes Cast in the Counties of New York, Bronx, Kings, Queens and Richmond at the Election Held November 7, 1933," *City Record*, LXI (December 30, 1933), 225. Hereafter referred to as *Official Canvass* (1933).

12. *Ibid.*, 222, 224, 225, 226.

13. *Ibid.*, 2, 15, 150.

14. Two election districts added to the Italian section of the 7th Assembly District in 1933 changed the boundaries of some of the election districts in question from those of 1932. But election district maps for both years reveal that the total area remained roughly the same, so that the comparison between La Guardia's and Roosevelt's returns is still valid. La Guardia's combined return from the two additional election districts, the Forty-ninth and Fiftieth, was 86.15 per cent. For the figures on which the percentages are based, see *Official Canvass* (1932), 95–96; *ibid.* (1933), 143.

15. *Il Progresso Italo-Americano*, November 8, 1933.

16. *Ibid.*

17. *Ibid.*

18. Charles P. Pinto to La Guardia, November 1, 1933, LGP. Very little has been written about the history of Italo-Americans in New York City. For a statistical study based on the census of 1930, see William B. Shedd, "Italian Population in New York" (Bulletin Number 7, Casa Italiana Educational Bureau: Columbia University, New York City, undated). The best survey is a book prepared by the Federal Writers' Project of the Works Progress Administration in New York City, *The Italians of New York* (New York, 1933).

19. Unidentified newspaper clipping (from Argentina), enclosed with George A. Kent to La Guardia, September 28, 1933, LGP; *Piccolo Giornale d'Italia,* quoted in *Il Progresso Italo-Americano,* November 9, 1933; Italo Balbo to La Guardia, October 16, 1933, LGP.

20. Galley proof of editorial, *Sons of Italy Magazine* (October–November, 1933), LGP.

21. *Il Minatore Italiano* (December 1, 1933), LGP.

22. *Il Progresso Italo-Americano,* October 22, November 5, 1933.

23. Edward Corsi to La Guardia, August 28, 1933, LGP; *Il Lazio,* August, October, 1933, *ibid.;* A. Mosca to La Guardia, August 9, 1933, *ibid.;* La Guardia to Mosca, September 5, 1933, *ibid.*

24. *Il Progresso Italo-Americano,* November 6, 1933.

25. Polling was then in its infancy, and the evidence from that source concerning the impact of the Jewish issue on the election is inconclusive. The New York *Daily News* and RKO Theaters polls revealed a falling off for McKee after the eruption of the anti-Semitic episode. See *Literary Digest,* CXVI (October 28, 1933), 7. But the poll conducted by the *Literary Digest,* which had La Guardia leading McKee from the latter's entry into the campaign until Election Day, reported a gain for McKee after the accusation that he was anti-Semitic. See *ibid.* (November 4, 1933), 7. None of the three polls isolated Jewish voters from others.

26. *American Hebrew and Jewish Tribune,* CXXXIII (November 3, 1933), 405.

27. *Morning Journal,* November 2, 8, 1932; November 6, 1933; *Day,* November 5, 1933; *Freiheit,* November 6, 1933; *Forward,* November 7, 8, 1933.

28. The eighteen assembly districts are the following: the Fourth, Sixth, Seventh, Eighth, Ninth, and Twenty-third in Manhattan; the Second, Third, Fifth, Sixth, and Seventh in the Bronx; Second, Sixth, Fourteenth, Sixteenth, Eighteenth, Twenty-second, and Twenty-third in Brooklyn. Hardly any Jews lived in Staten Island, and the Rockaway election districts in Queens are the 123rd, 124th, and 129th in the Fifth Assembly District.

29. Hillquit's death in 1933 rated a front-page obituary in the New York *Times* of October 19. For his credo and his position in the Socialist Party, see his *Loose Leaves from a Busy Life* (New York, 1934). Cf. David A. Shannon, *The Socialist Party of America* (New York, 1955), 211–217; Daniel Bell, "The Background of Marxian Socialism in the United States," in Donald D. Egbert and Stow Persons, eds., *Socialism and American Life* (Princeton, 1952), II, 377–378.

30. Moses Rischin, *The Promised City, New York's Jews: 1870–
1914* (Cambridge, 1962), 76–94 and *passim; New York City Market
Analysis,* "Manhattan 3"; C. Morris Horowitz, Lawrence J. Kaplan,
The Jewish Population of the New York Area, 1900–1975 (New
York, 1959), 26.

31. For similar views of the voting habits of the native American
middle classes and the immigrant poor, see Oscar Handlin, *The
Uprooted* (Boston, 1953), 201–226; Richard Hofstadter, *The Age
of Reform* (New York, 1955), 131 ff.; Edward C. Banfield,
James Q. Wilson, *City Politics* (Cambridge, 1963), 115–127, 138–
150, 229–242, 329–346. These and other recent scholars were anticipated by such older writers as James Bryce and M. I. Ostrogorski in, respectively, *The American Commonwealth* (1888) and
Democracy and the Organization of Political Parties (1902).

32. For typical returns by precinct from Central Park West see
those from the 21st, 25th, and 36th election districts in the Seventh
Assembly District, and the 48th, 49th, and 50th election districts in
the Ninth Assembly District, *Official Canvass* (1933), 9, 10. "Manhattan 13" in *New York City Market Analysis* contains a visual
and statistical description of the area in terms of income, nativity,
and housing.

33. See, for example, the returns in the Second Assembly District from 112th through 115th election districts, *Official Canvass*
(1933), 133.

34. *Ibid.,* 326 (see especially the returns from the 123rd, 124th,
129th, 131st, and 132nd election districts in the Fifth Assembly District).

35. *Ibid.,* 225 (compare the returns from the predominantly
Jewish election districts in the Fourteenth—1, 10, 11, 12, 13, 14, 15,
16, 18, 19, 20, 21, 24, and 25—with those from the preponderantly
Italian 6th, 7th, 8th, 17th, 22nd, 27th, and 28th election districts).

36. *Ibid.,* 230. For Italian returns in the Twenty-third, see election districts 3 through 10, and for Jewish returns election districts
13 through 24.

37. See, for example, the returns from election districts 17
through 22 in the Second Assembly District; 87 through 92 in
the Eighteenth Assembly District; 82 through 88 in the Twenty-
first Assembly District, *ibid.,* 218, 228, 229.

38. For typical Jewish returns from the Sixteenth Assembly
District, see election districts 1 through 5 and 23 through 27; and
for Italian returns election districts 49, 62, 63, 95, 125, 126, 129, 130,
131, 136, 137, *ibid.,* 225–226.

39. This estimate is based on both *New York City Market Analysis* and Horowitz and Kaplan, *The Jewish Population of the New
York Area, 1900–1975.*

40. Ed Flynn, *You're the Boss* (New York, 1947), 137; Eleanor

Ernst, "Fusion Campaign Methods in the New York Fusion Mayoralty Campaign of 1933" (Smith College Honors Thesis, 1934), 128.

CHAPTER VI

The Meaning of the Mandate:
"The Brains of Tammany Hall Lie in Calvary Cemetery"

1. Walter Laidlaw, *Population of the City of New York, 1890–1930* (New York, 1932), 275.

2. For similar views about Jews and Protestants in anti-boss movements, see Daniel P. Moynihan, "Bosses and Reformers," *Commentary*, XXXI (June, 1961), 461–470; Theodore J. Lowi, *At the Pleasure of the Mayor: Patronage and Power in New York City, 1898–1958* (New York, 1964), especially 36, 38, 197–199; Richard Skolnik, "The Crystallization of Reform in New York City, 1890–1917" (unpublished Ph.D. dissertation, Yale University, 1964), 22–54, 386–387, and *passim*; James Q. Wilson, *The Amateur Democrat: Club Politics in Three Cities* (Chicago, 1962), 2–58, 265–267, and *passim*.

3. Oswald Garrison Villard to La Guardia, August 28, 1933, LGP.

4. The quotations come, in order of appearance, from the New York *Daily News*, November 8, 1933; New York *Herald Tribune*, November 8, 1933; Reuben A. Lazarus, *Reminiscences* (Oral History Project, Columbia University, 1949–1951), 169–170.

5. Quoted in Gene Fowler, *The Life & Times of Jimmy Walker, Beau James* (New York, 1949), 11. For two illuminating assessments of Murphy's talents, see J. Joseph Huthmacher, "Charles Evans Hughes and Charles Francis Murphy: The Metamorphosis of Progressivism," *New York History*, XLVI (January, 1965), 25–40; Nancy J. Weiss, "Charles Francis Murphy, 1858–1924: Respectability and Responsibility in Tammany Politics" (Smith College Honors Thesis, 1965).

6. Adolf A. Berle to Arthur Mann, March 31, 1965.

Index

Fusion (*cont.*)
87; 1933 campaign, 89, 92–94,
101, 102, 103–04, 106, 113, 117,
118; analysis of returns, 123–
59. *See also* La Guardia, 1933
campaign
Fusioneers, 99–100, 102, 119

Gannet, Lewis, 70
Garner, Vice-President John
N., 67n
German-Americans, 42, 110,
112, 132, 133, 135, 144, 149
George, Henry, 41–42
Gibboni, 78, 78n
Godkin, E. L., 47
Goo Goos, 41, 68, 69, 83, 88,
107, 108, 155
Good Government Associa-
tions, 41, 67, 68, 81, 88, 104,
106
Gottlieb, Maurice, 57–58
Graft, *honest* and *dishonest*, 52–
53, 54, 57. *See also* Seabury
Investigations; Tammany
Hall

Harriman, W. Averell, 97
Harvey, George U., 93
Hearst, William Randolph, 40,
43
Hickin, William H., 56
Hillquit, Morris, 64, in 1932
election, 63–64, 142–55 *passim*
Hitler, Adolf, 16, 23, 75, 110,
112, 114, 137, 150
Holmes, Reverend John
Haynes, 99
Honest Ballot Association, 99,
102, 119
Hoover, Herbert H., 24n, 120;

in 1932 election, 126–52
passim
Howard, Roy, 19, 73, 85, 88, 97,
154
Howe, Ben, 82–83, 101
Hungarian-Americans, 75
Hylan, Mayor "Red Mike," 60,
69

Immigrants. *See* Ethnic groups
Independent Labor Party, 42
Independent voters, 96, 105
Ingersoll, Raymond V., 79, 93–
94
Intellectuals, and La Guardia,
32, 108–09, 155
Irish-Americans, 25, 42, 49, 69,
92, 110, 132, 133, 144, 145, 148,
149
Irish-American League for Fusion, 100
Isaacs, Stanley, 77, 86, 88
Italo-Americans, 18, 25, 26, 45,
75, 82–83, 87, 92, 110, 136, 140;
desert Democratic Party to
support La Guardia, 71, 78,
80, 99–100, 102–03, 108, 119;
votes swing election to La
Guardia, 127, 129–38, 144, 145,
148, 149, 152, 155, 159. *See also*
Press, Italian
Italian Fusion Committee, 134,
138

Jews, 26, 68, 79, 92, 110, 125, 132,
133; and La Guardia, 16, 25–
26, 75, 112–16, 137, 159; split
along class lines in 1933, 138–
52. *See also* Anti-Semitism;
Press, Jewish

Kelly, John, 47, 48n, 49